Anno's Animals
MITSUMASA ANNO

THE BODLEY HEAD
London · Sydney · Toronto

ISBN 0-370-30213-3
Copyright © Fukuinkan Shoten Publishers, Tokyo, 1977
Printed and bound in Great Britain for
The Bodley Head Ltd, 9 Bow Street, London, WC2E 7AL
by William Clowes & Sons Ltd, Beccles and London
First published in Japan as Anno's Strange Woods 1977
First published in Great Britain 1979

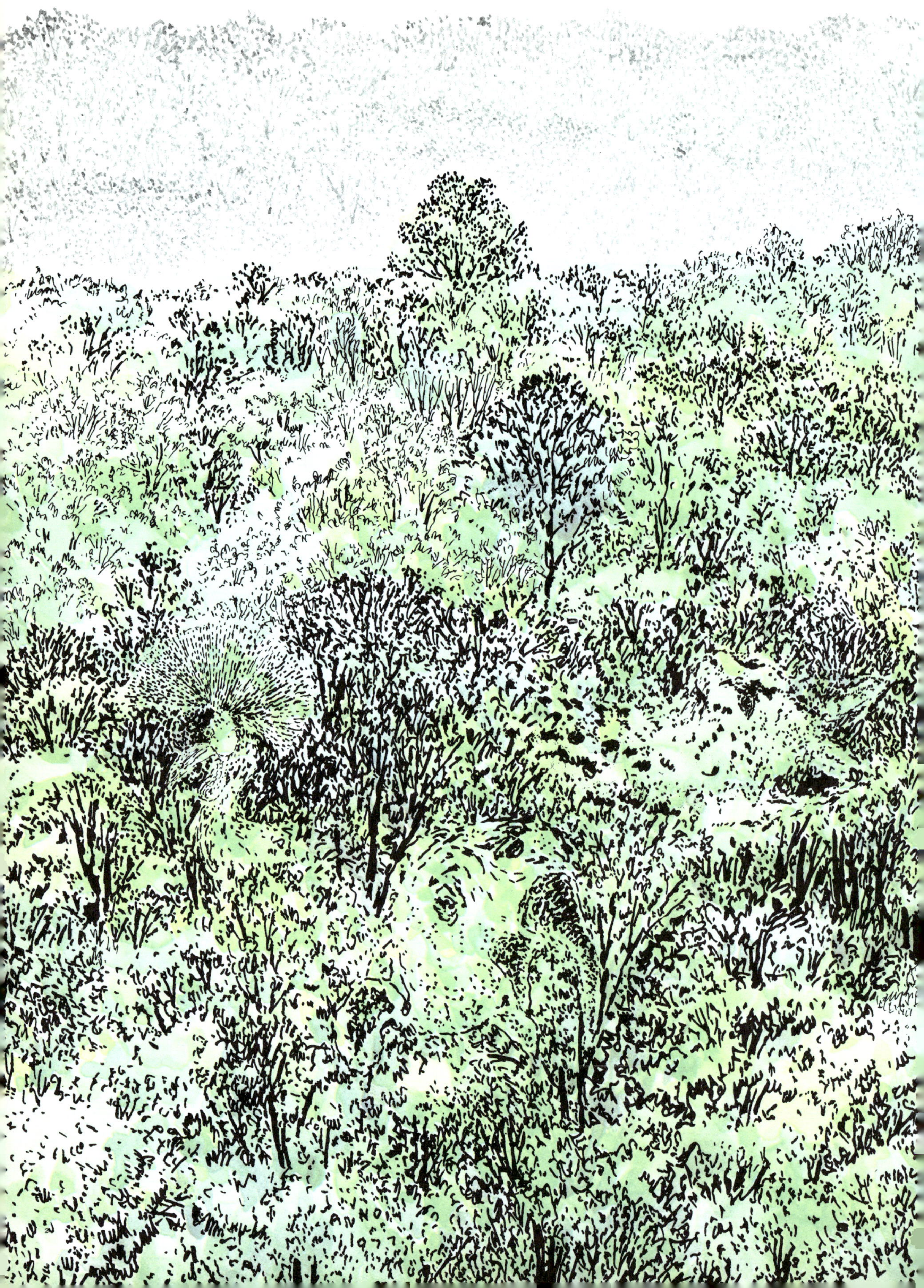

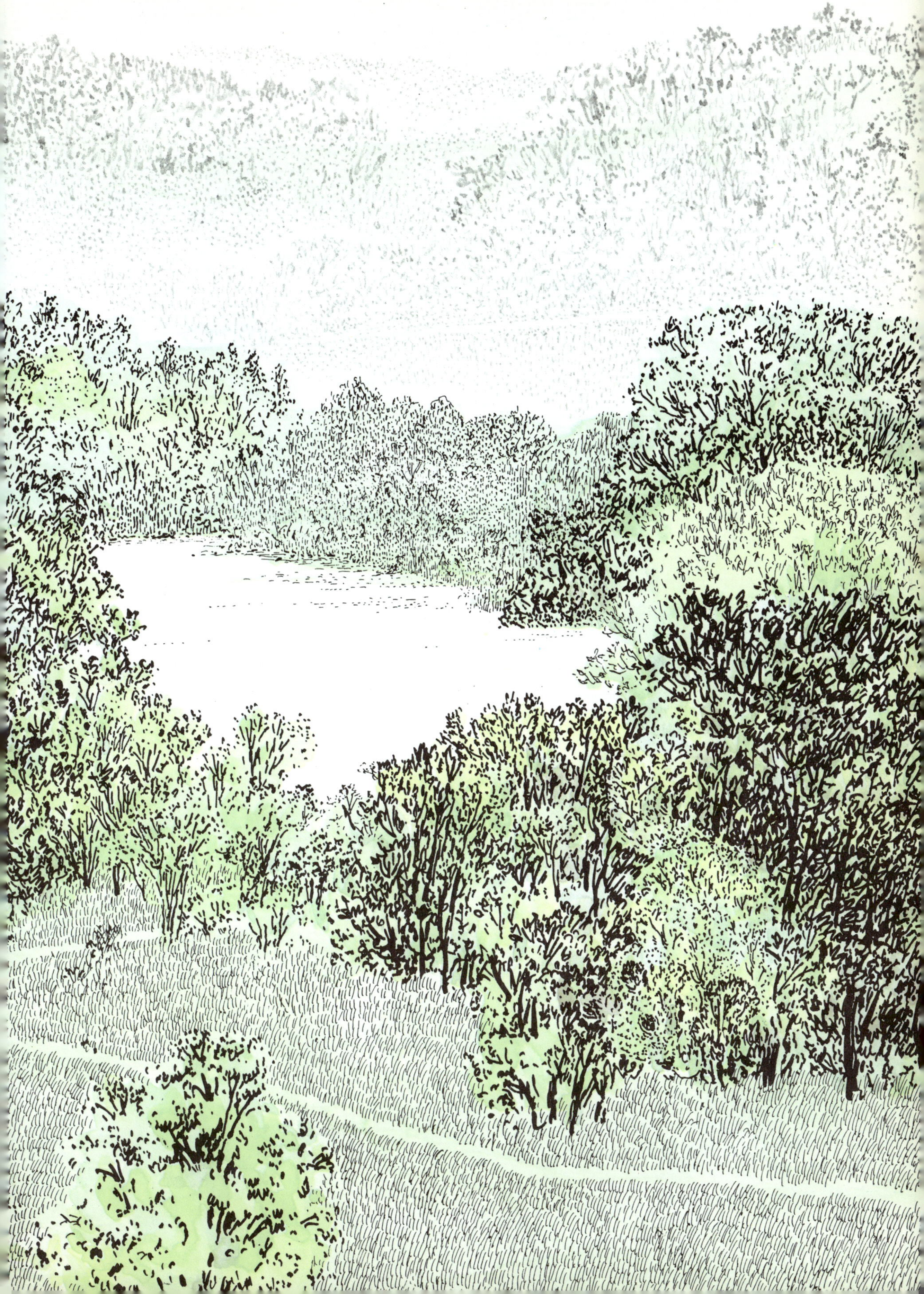

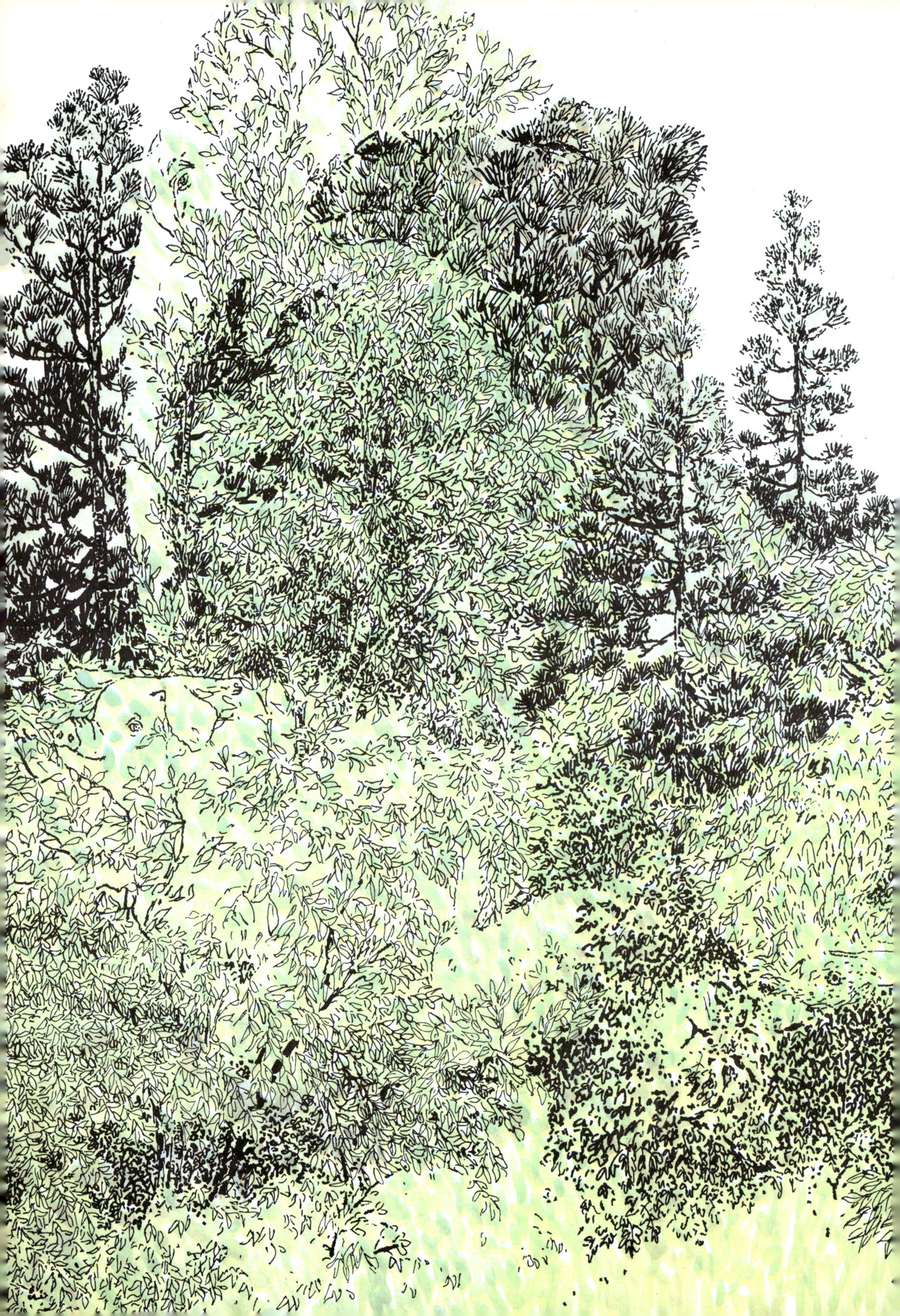

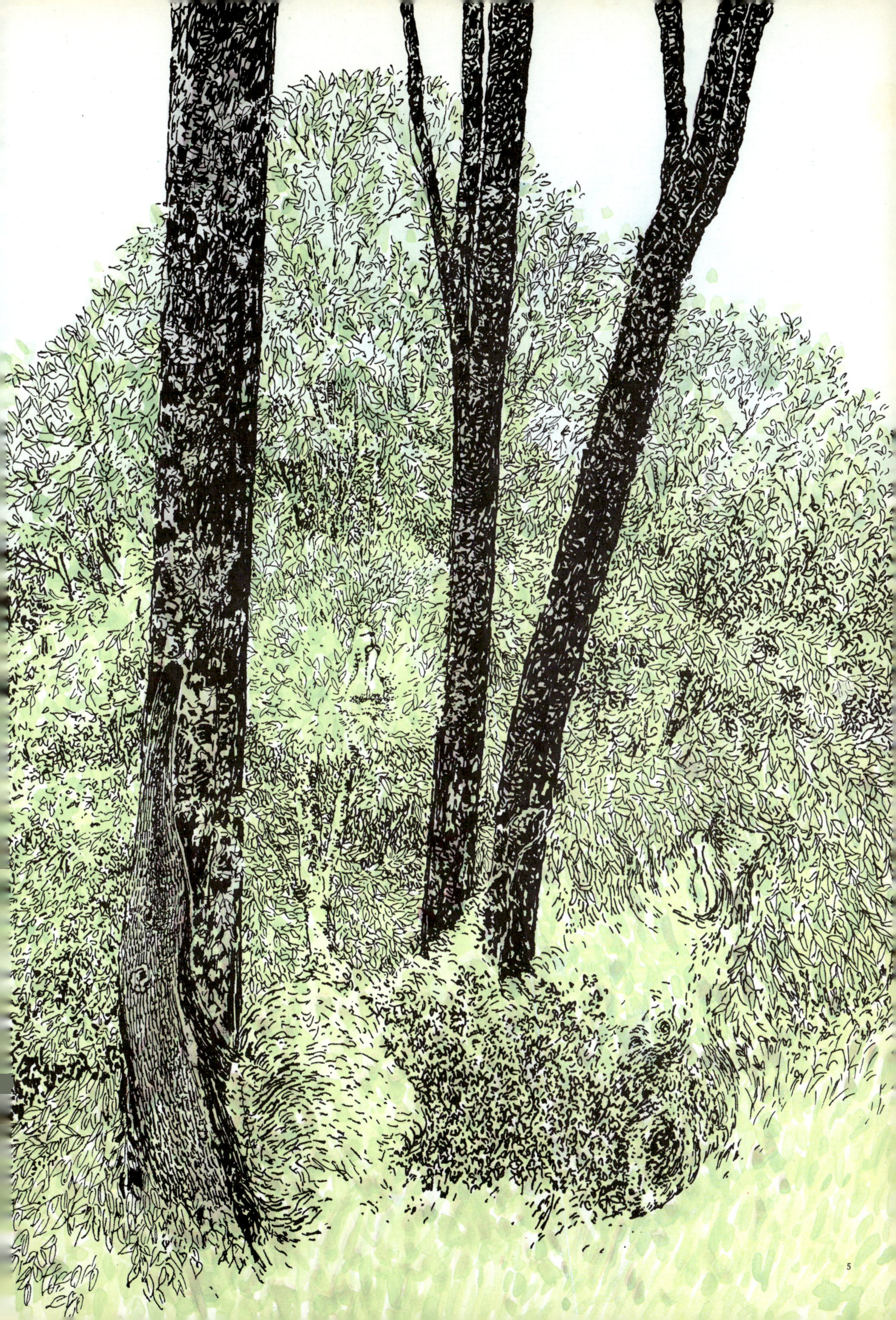

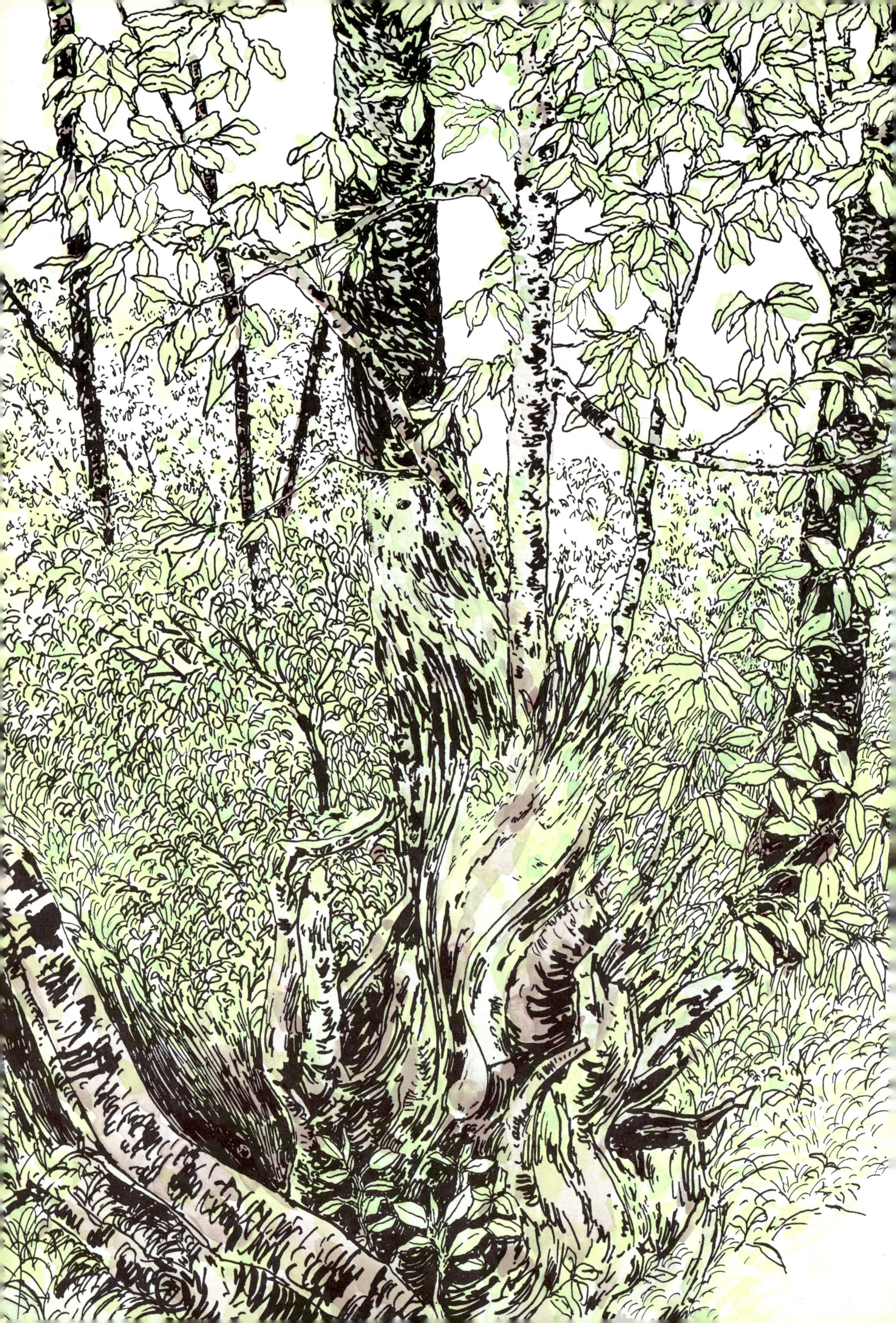

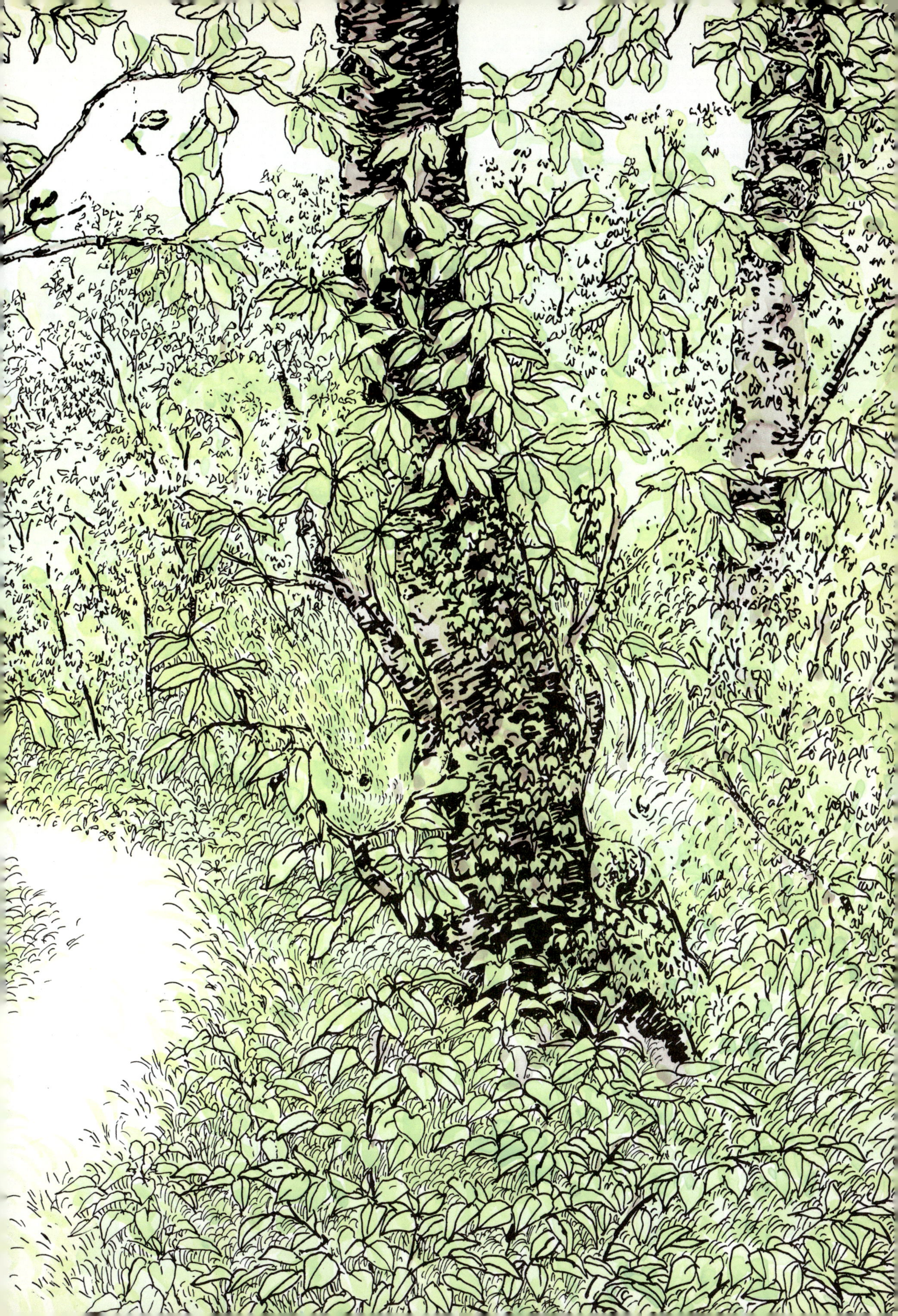

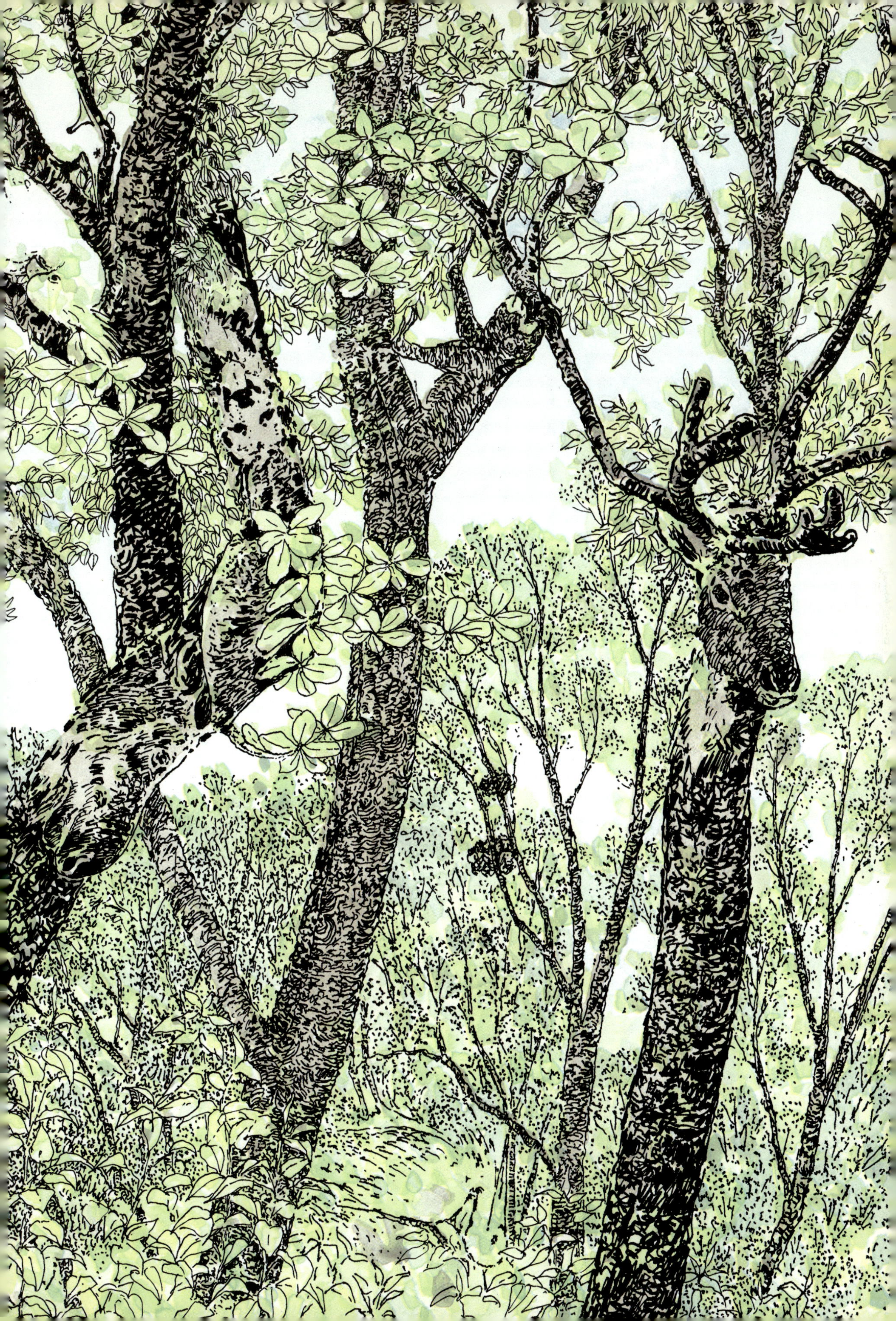

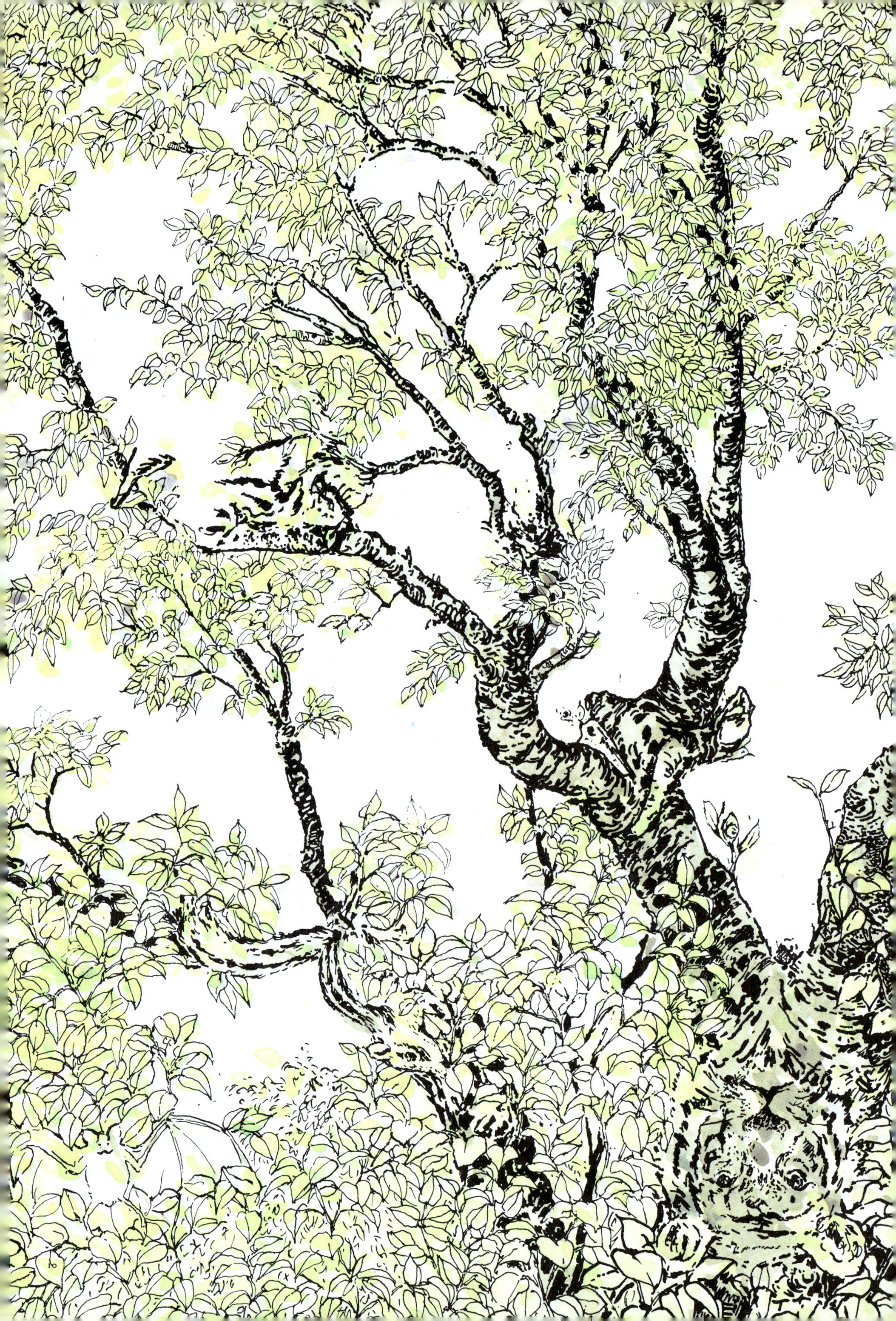

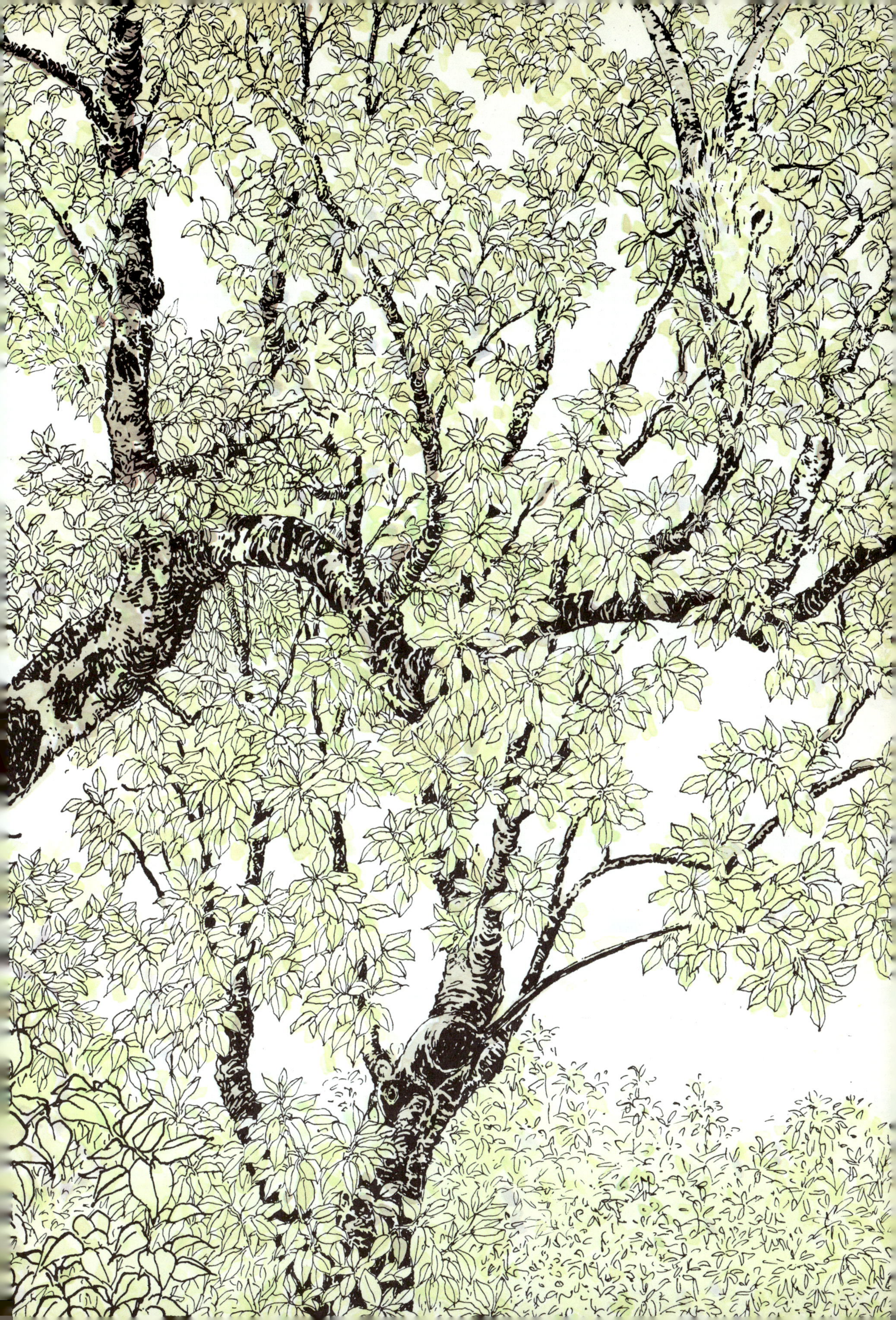

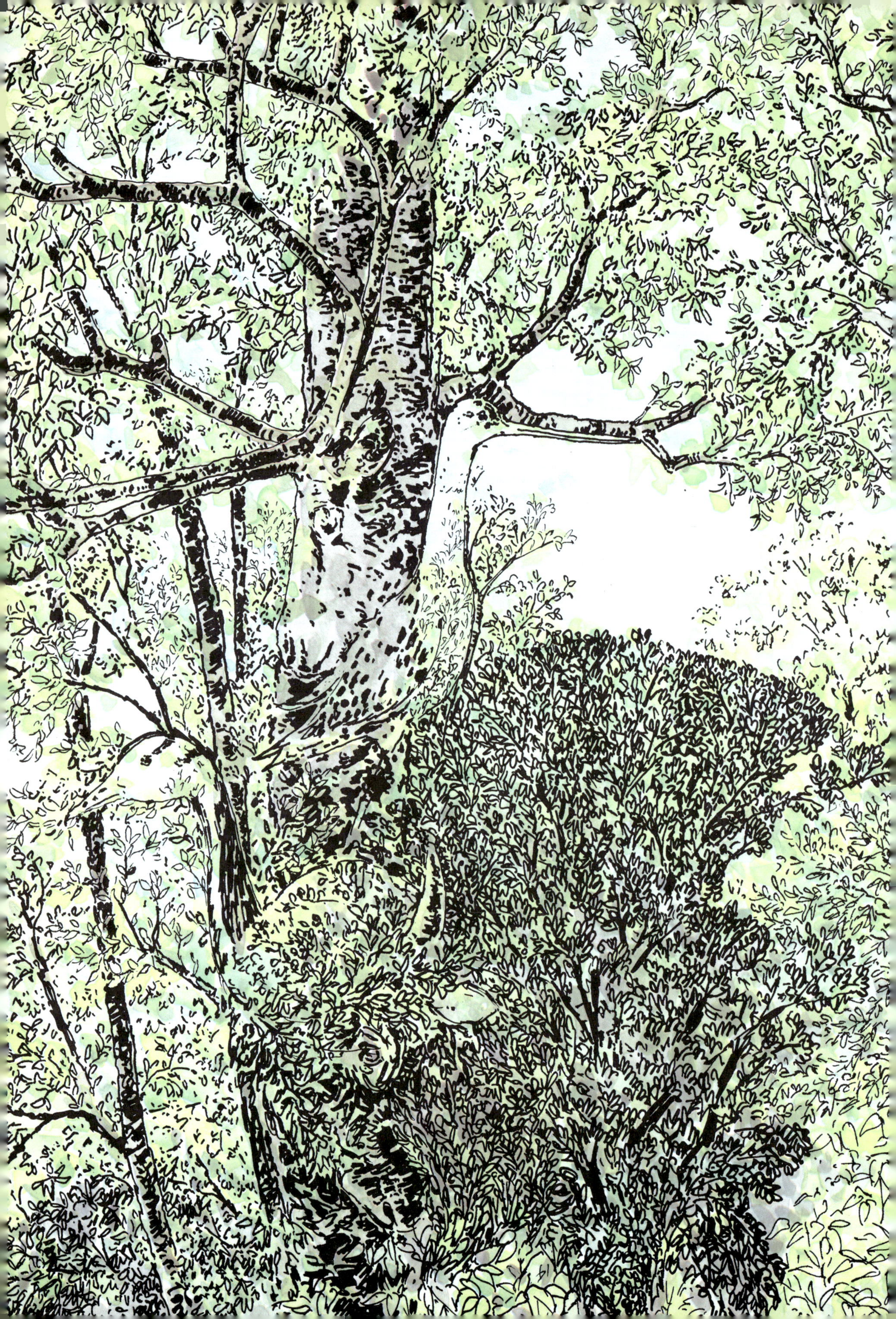

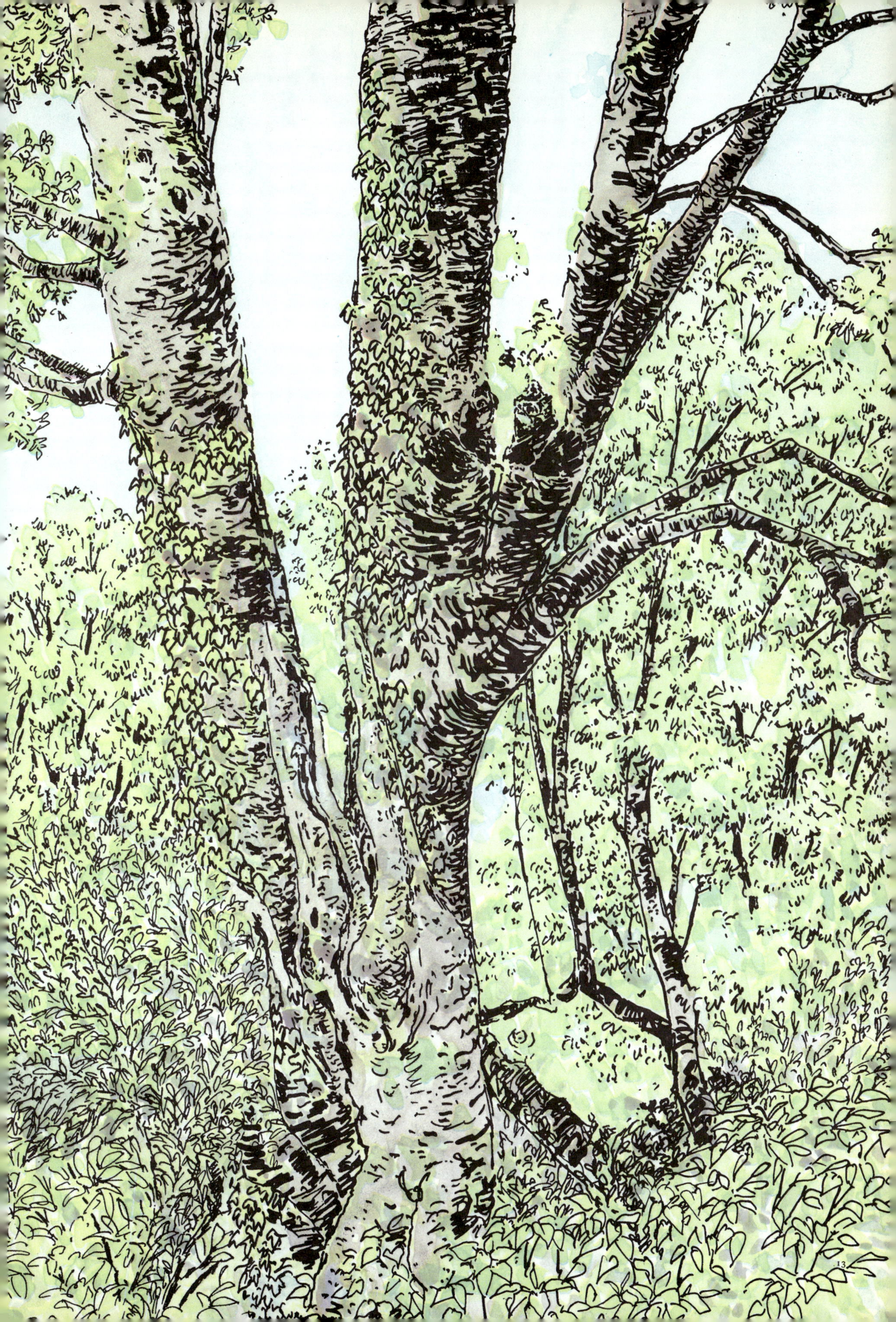

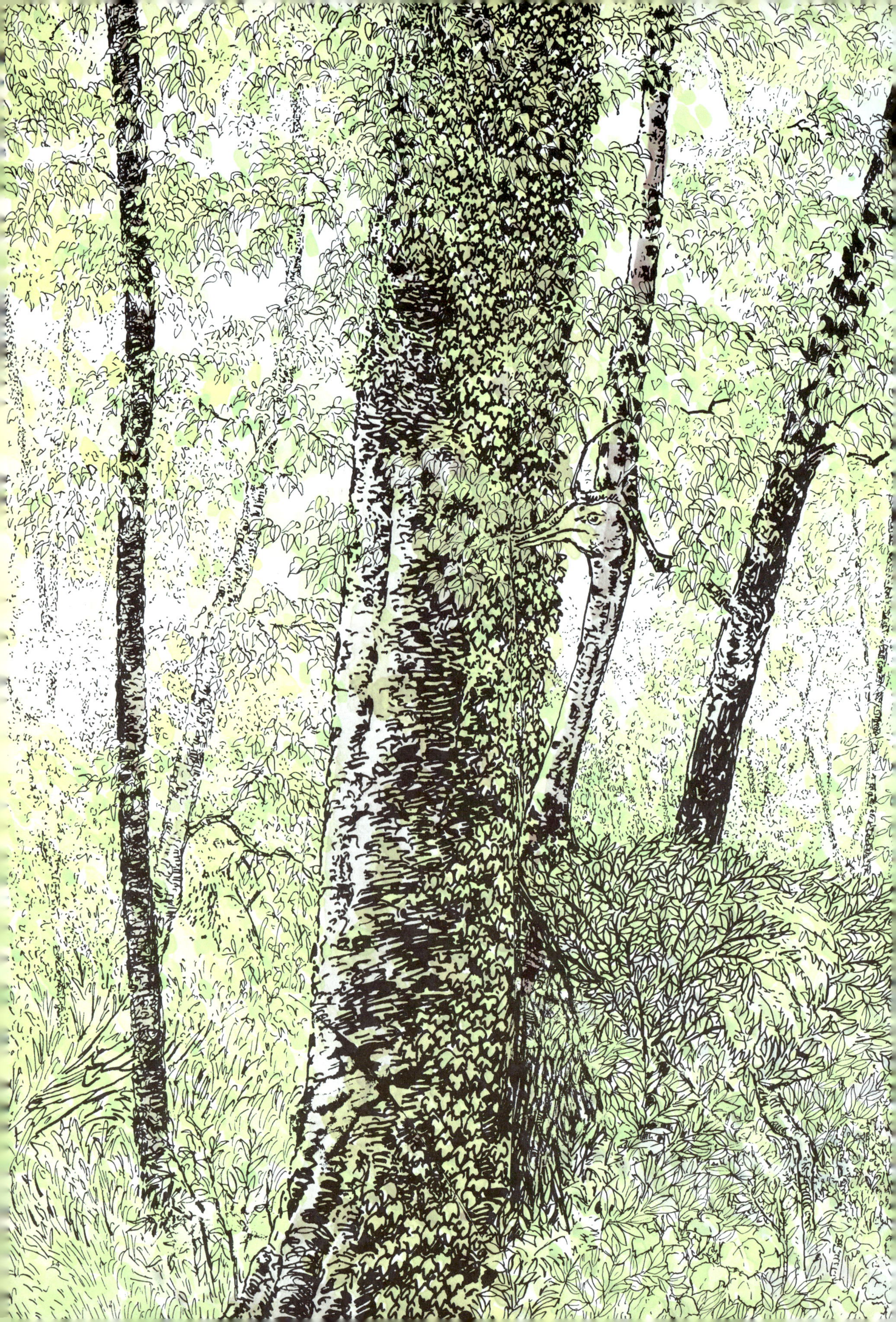

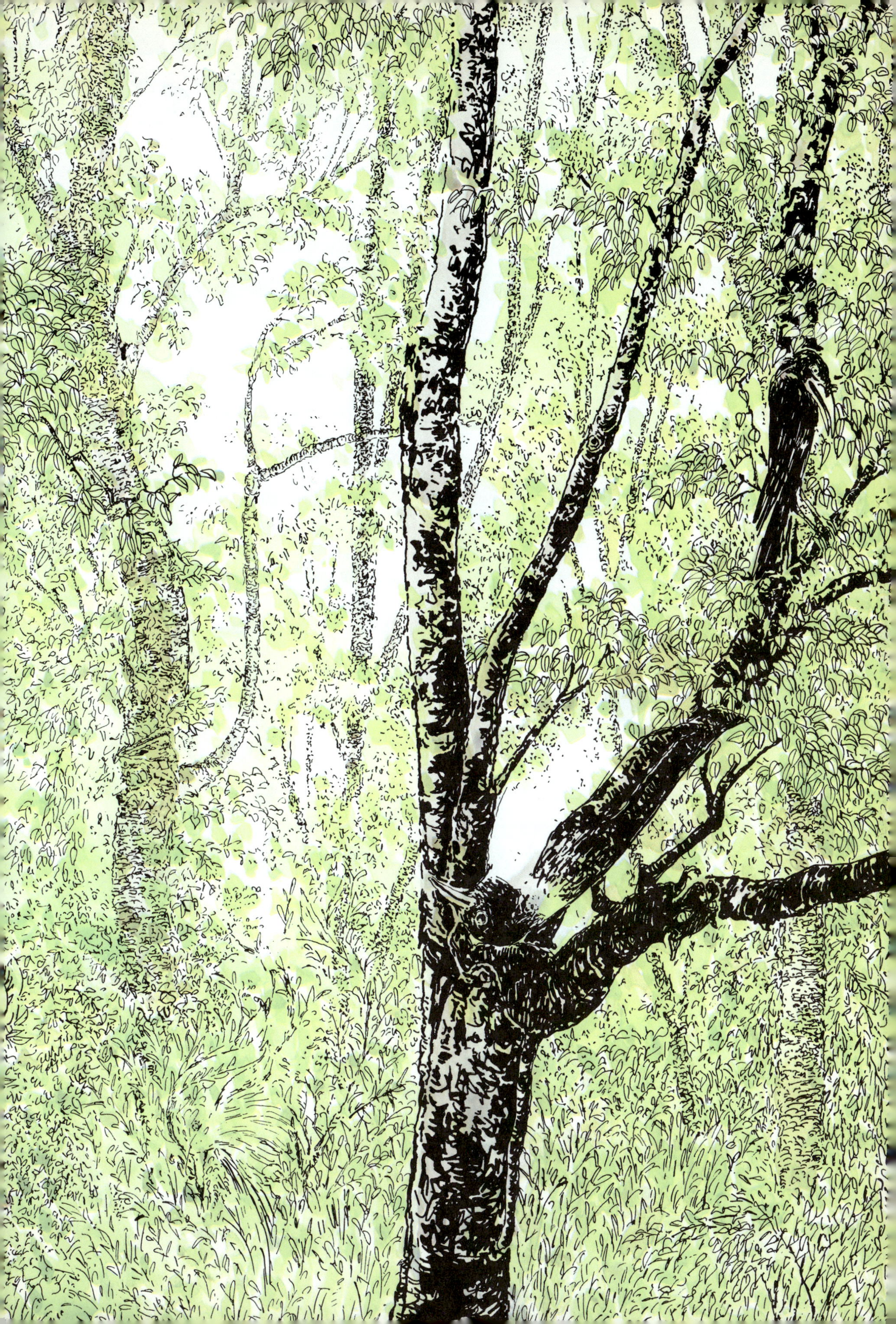

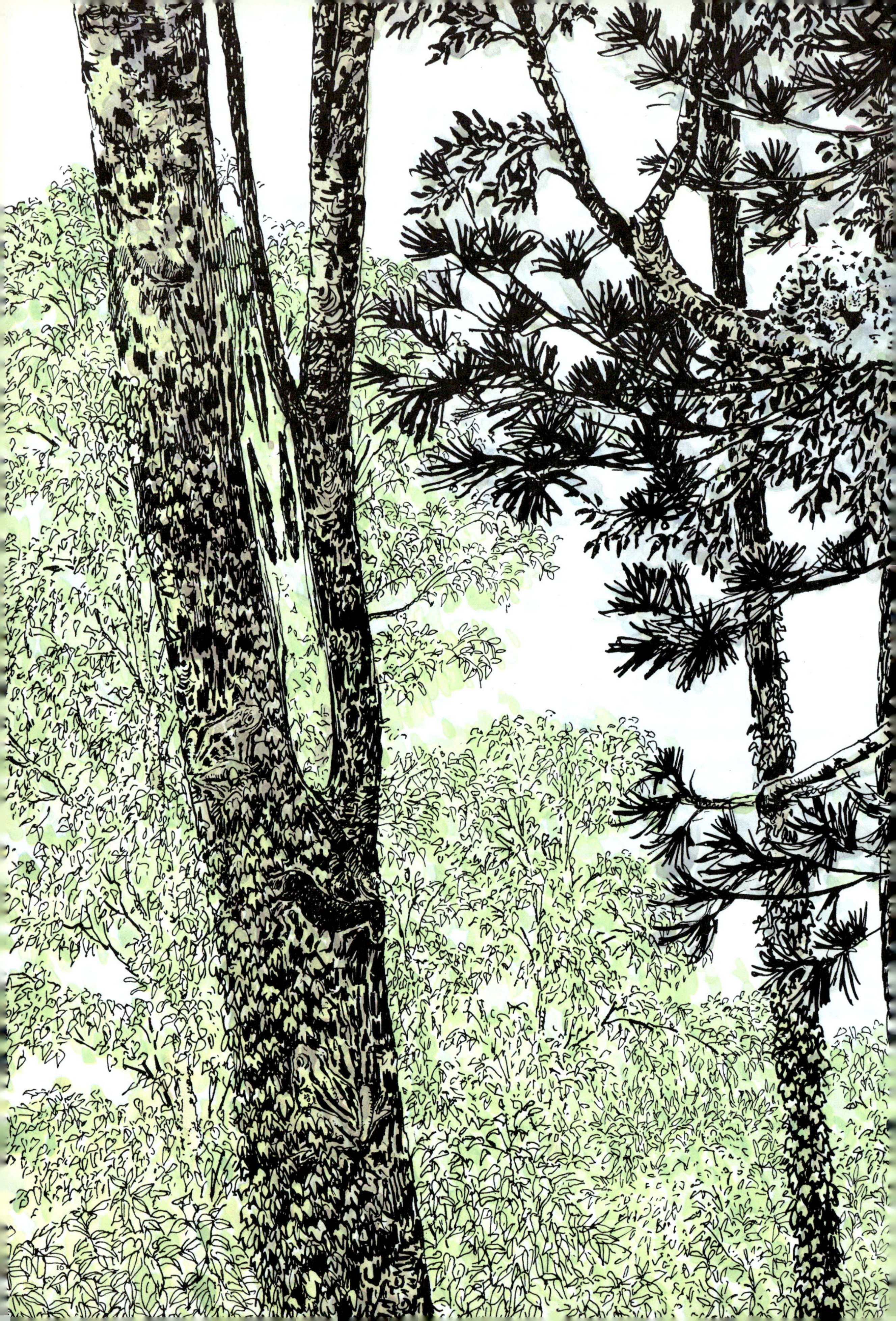

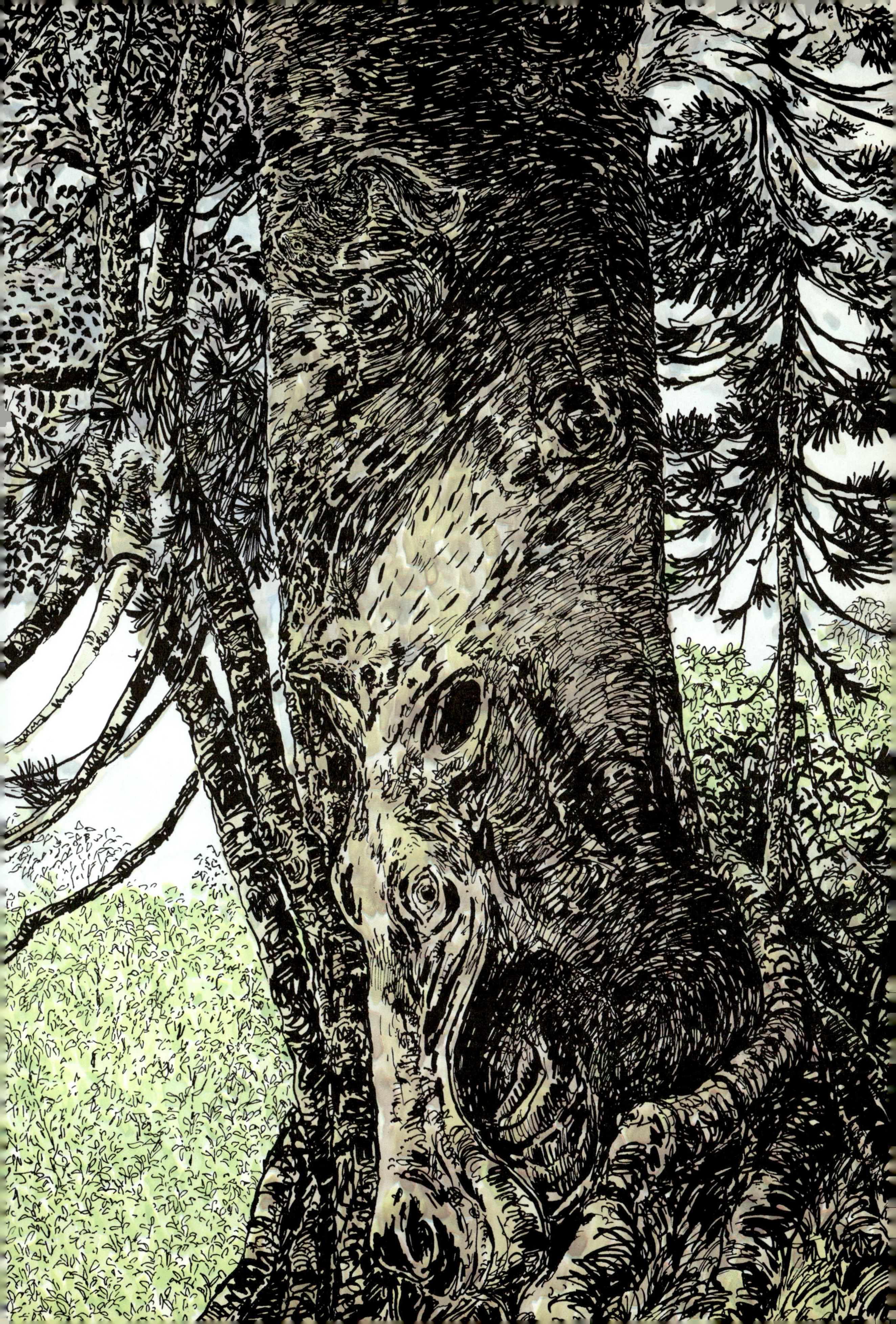

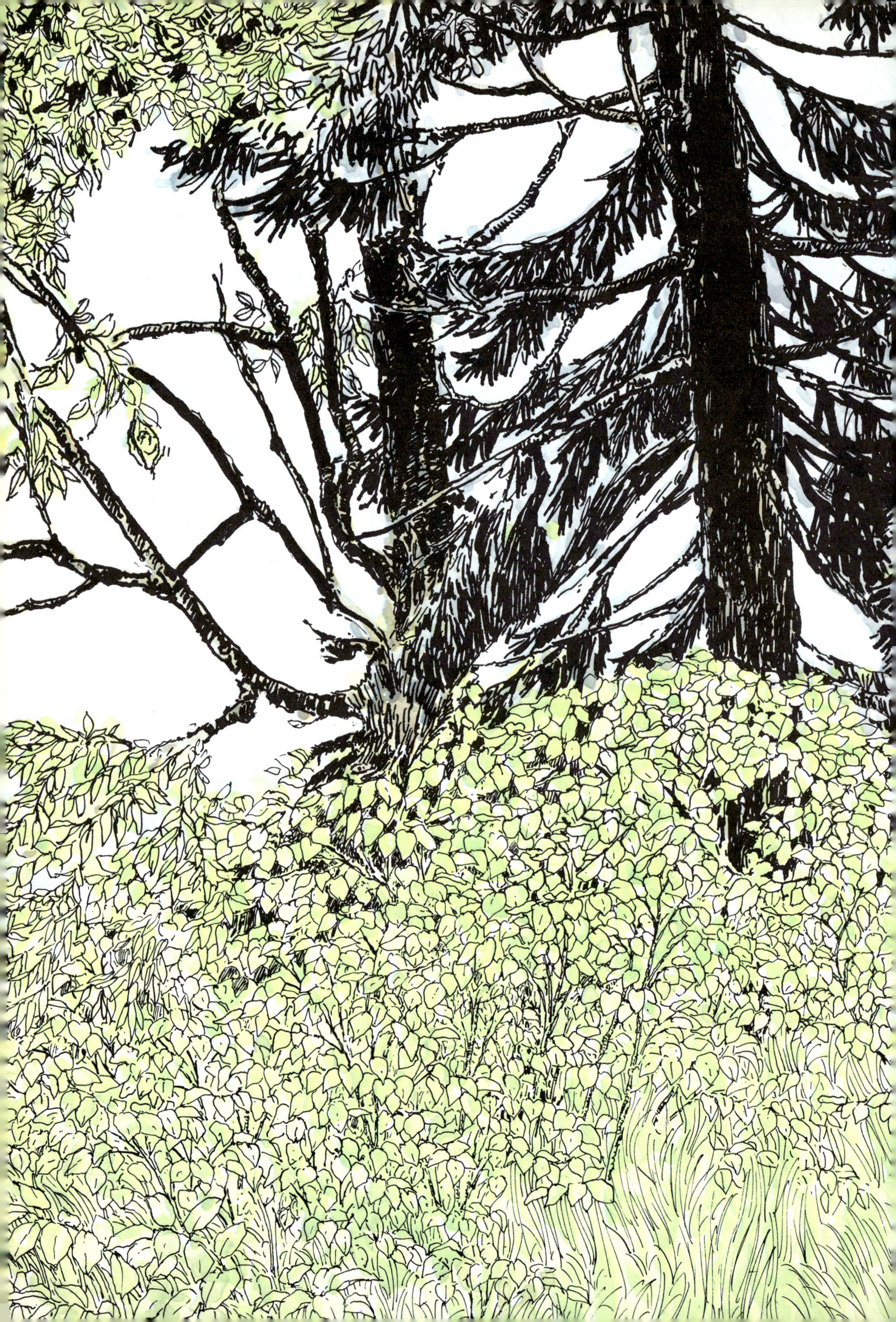

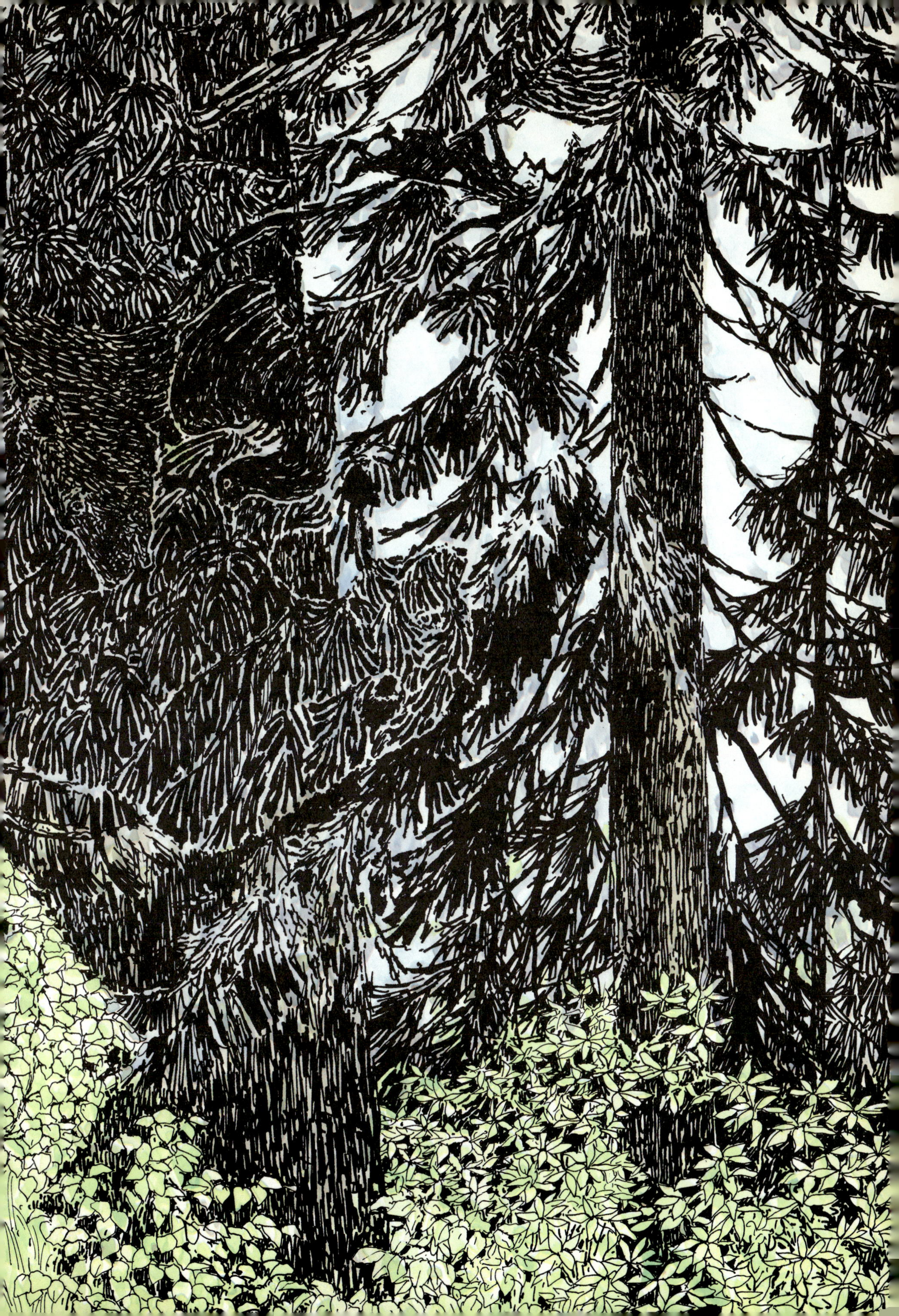

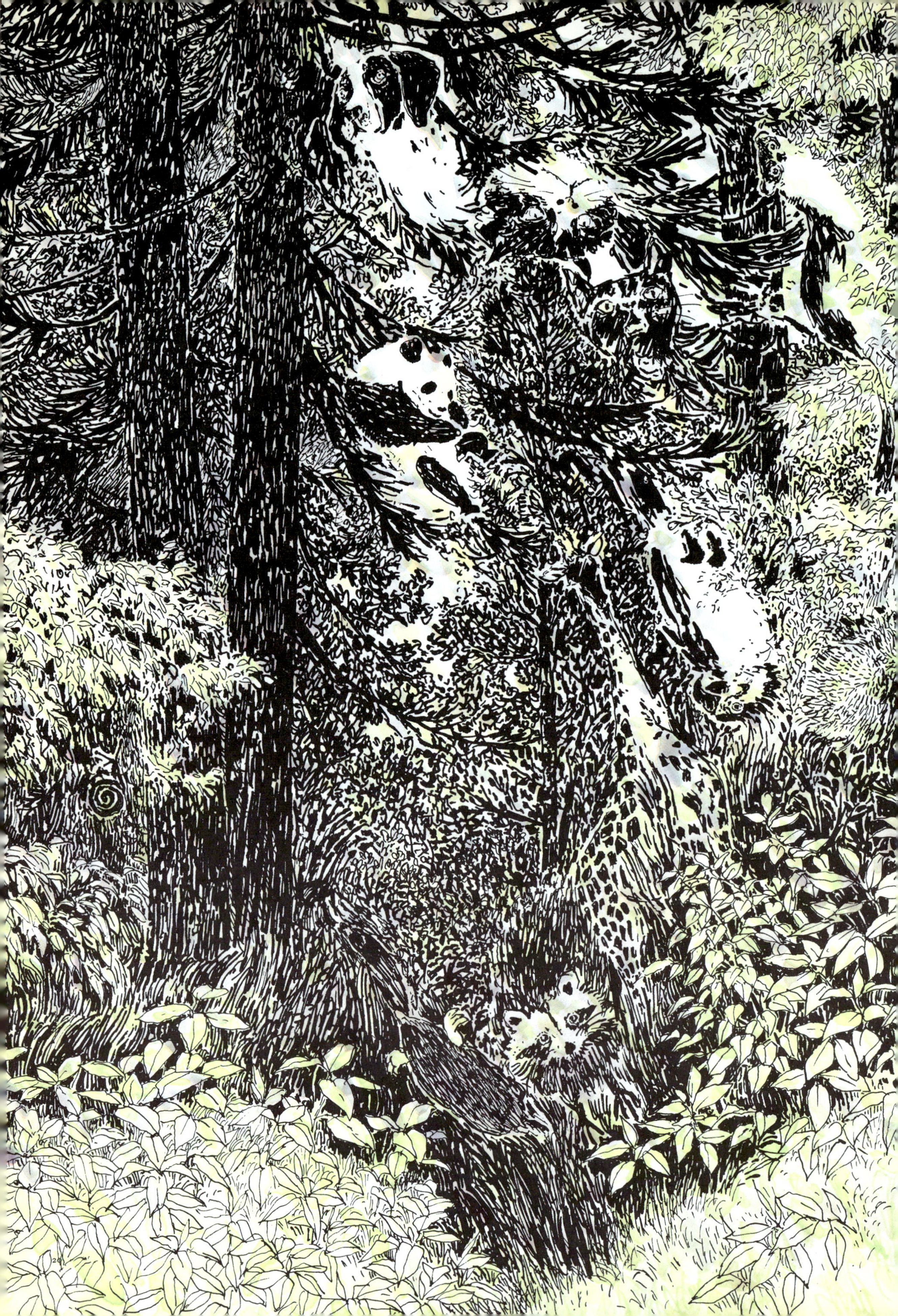

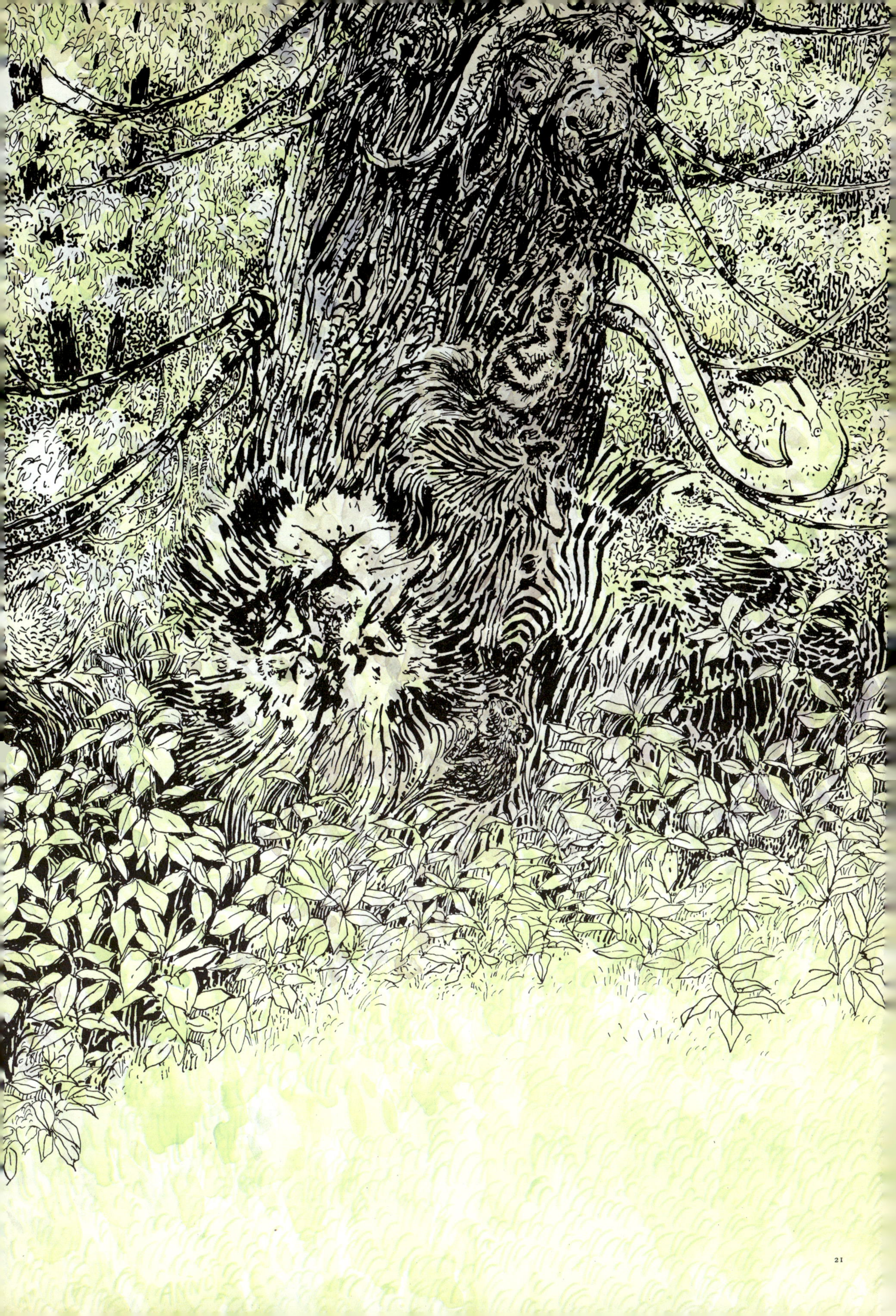

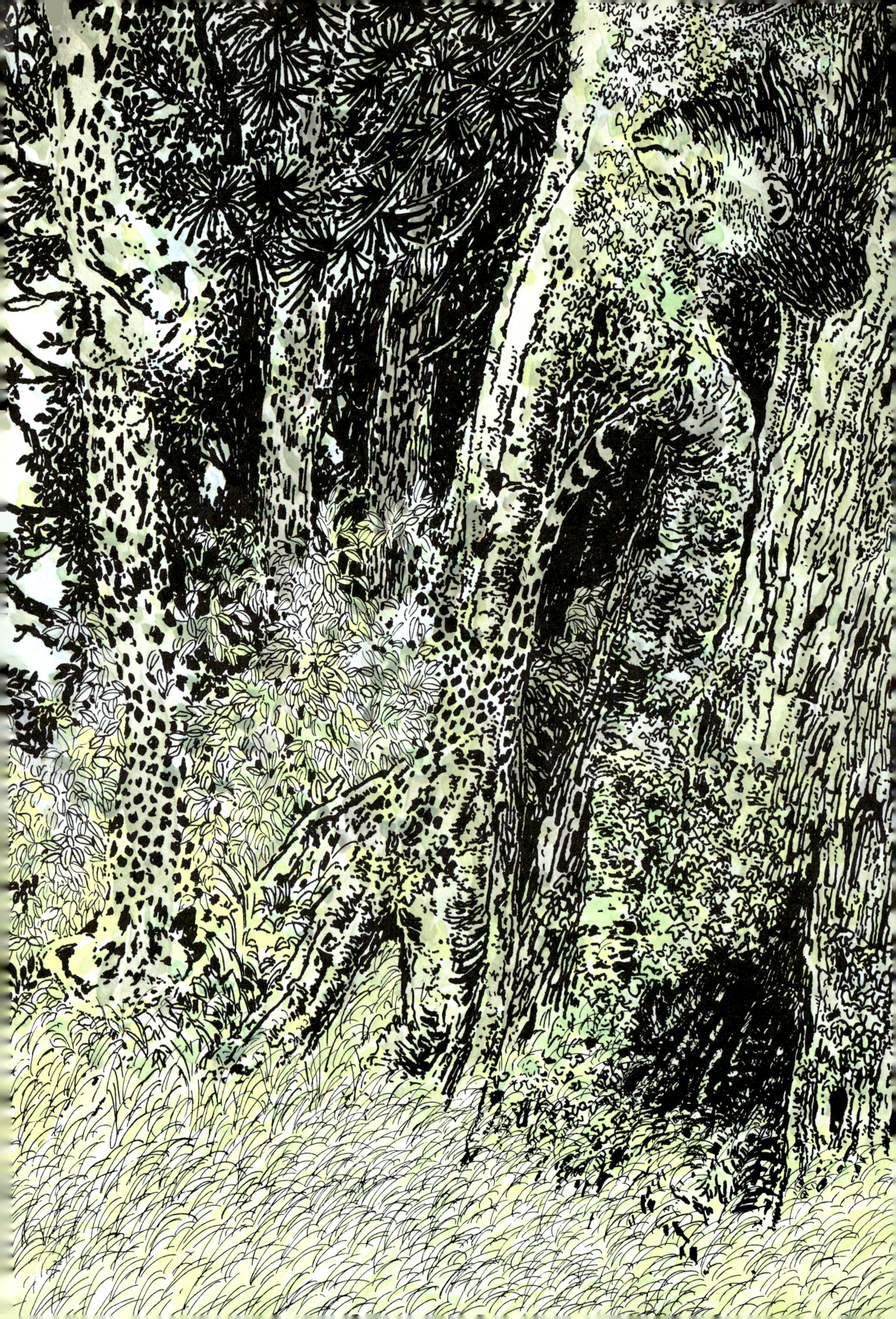

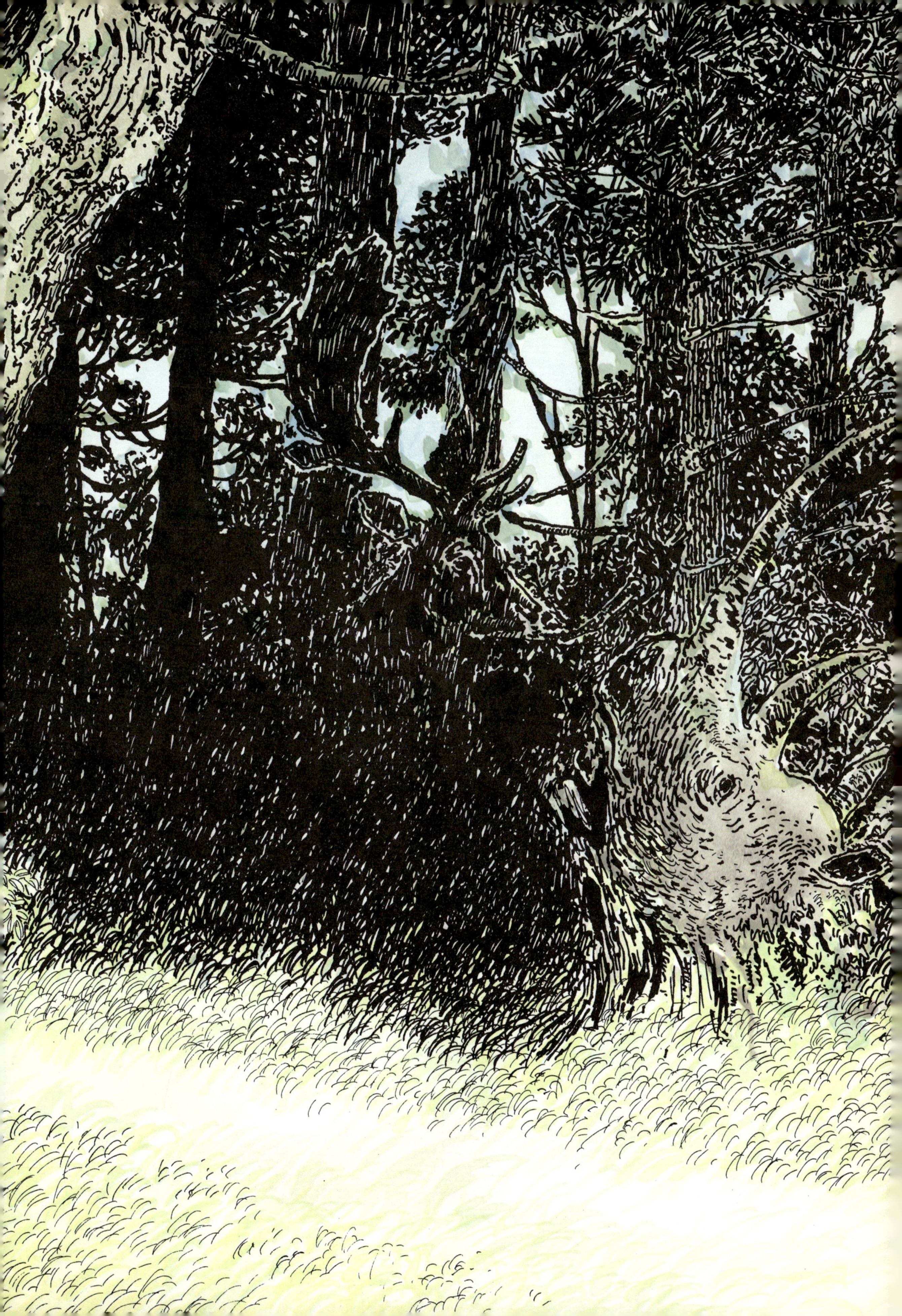

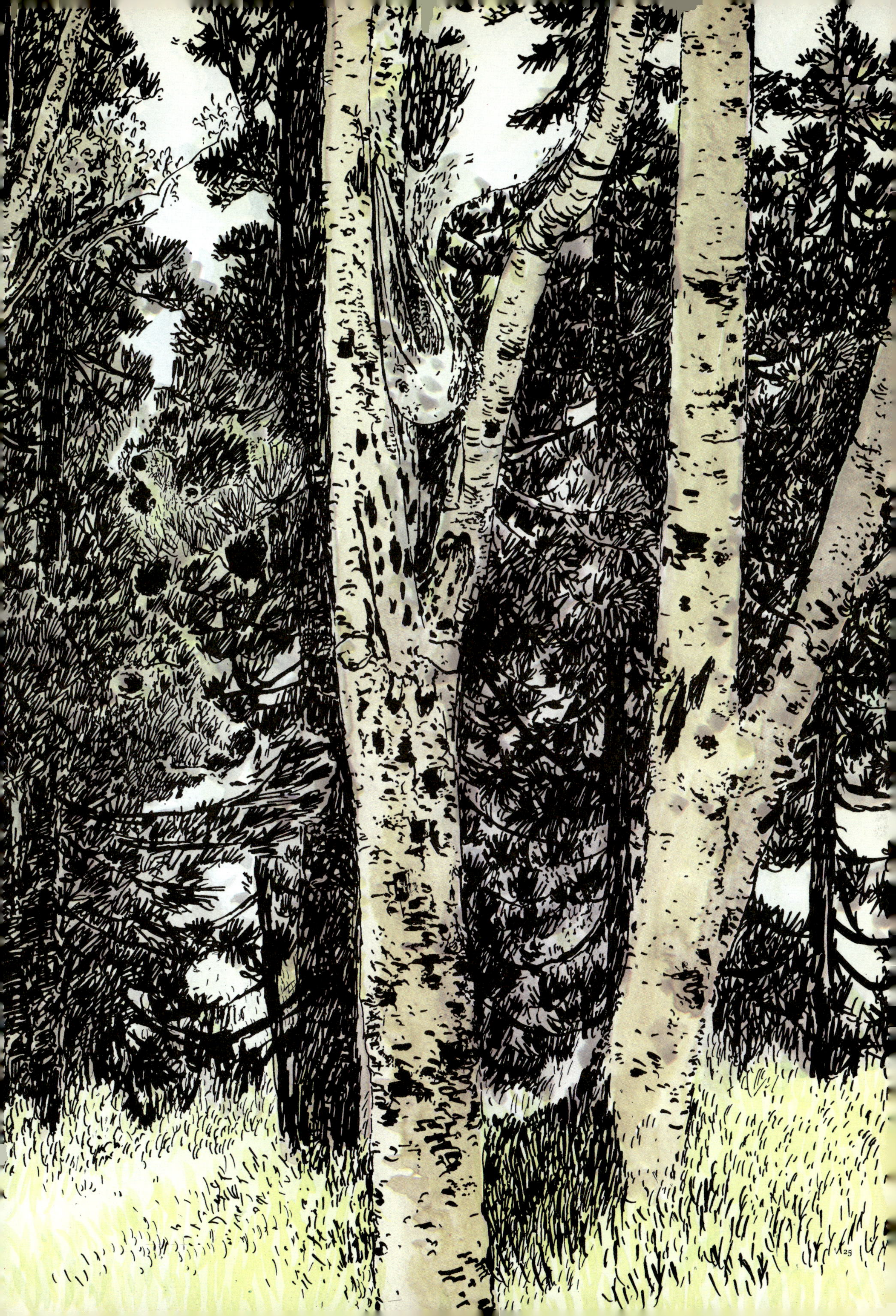

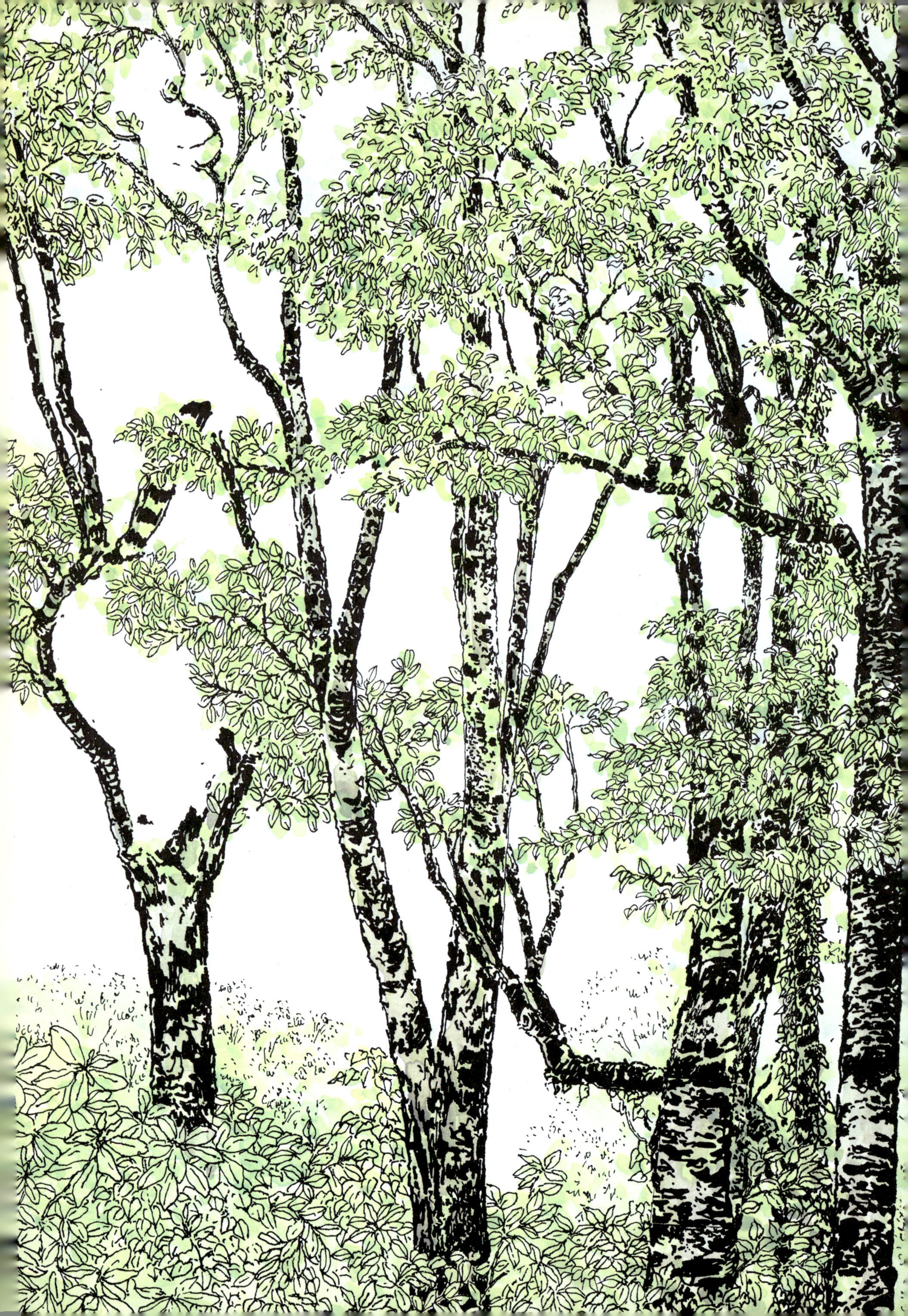

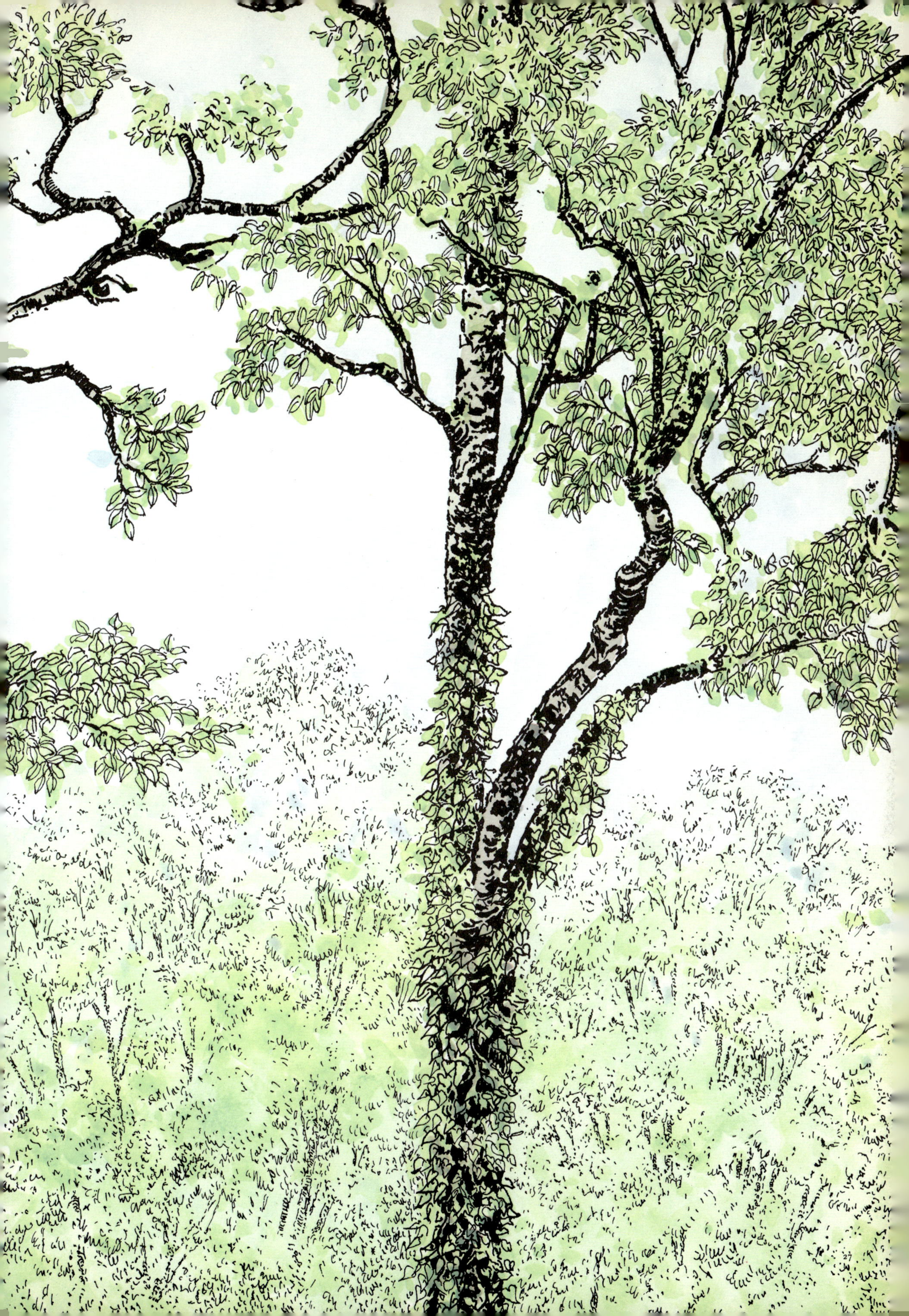

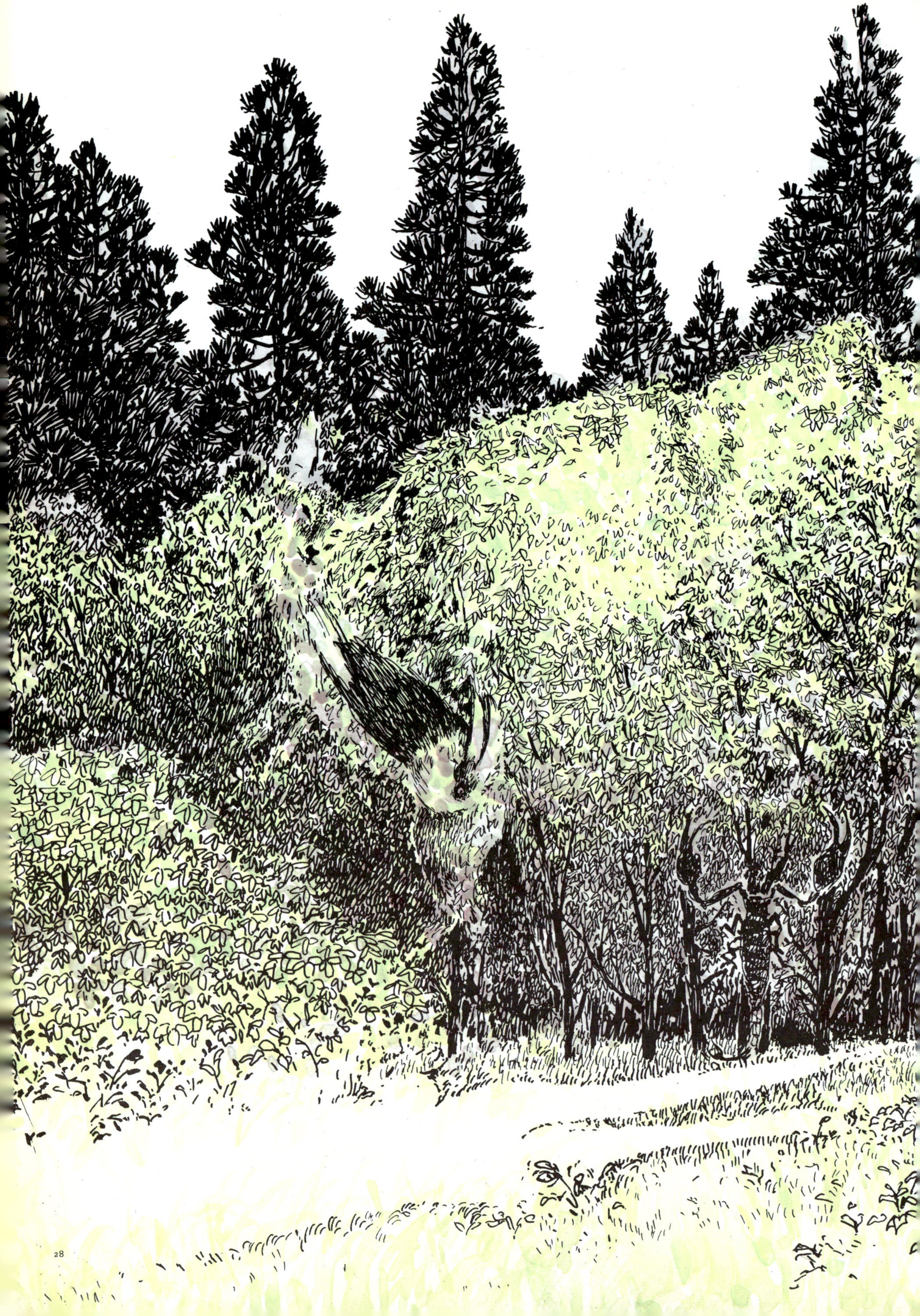

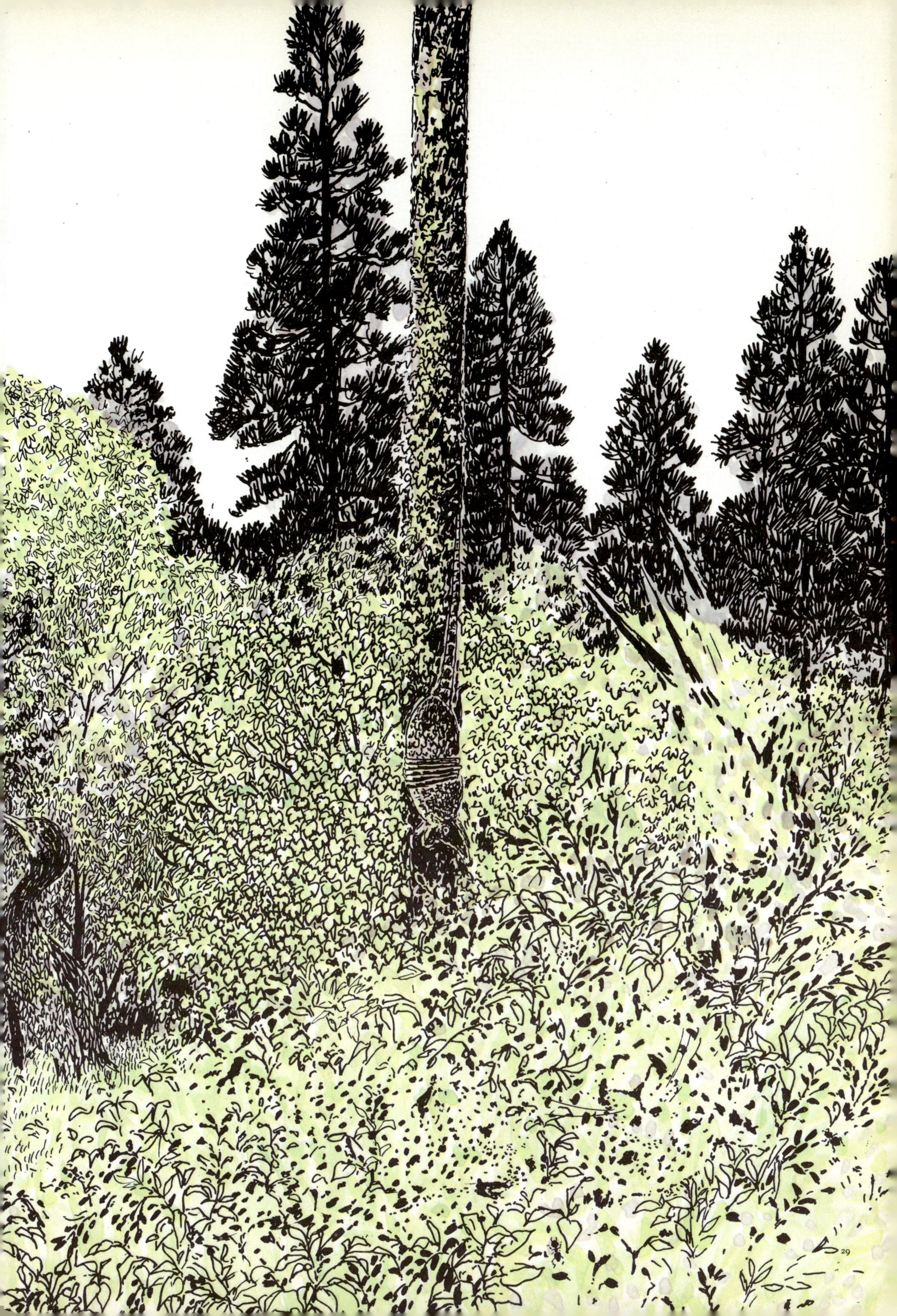

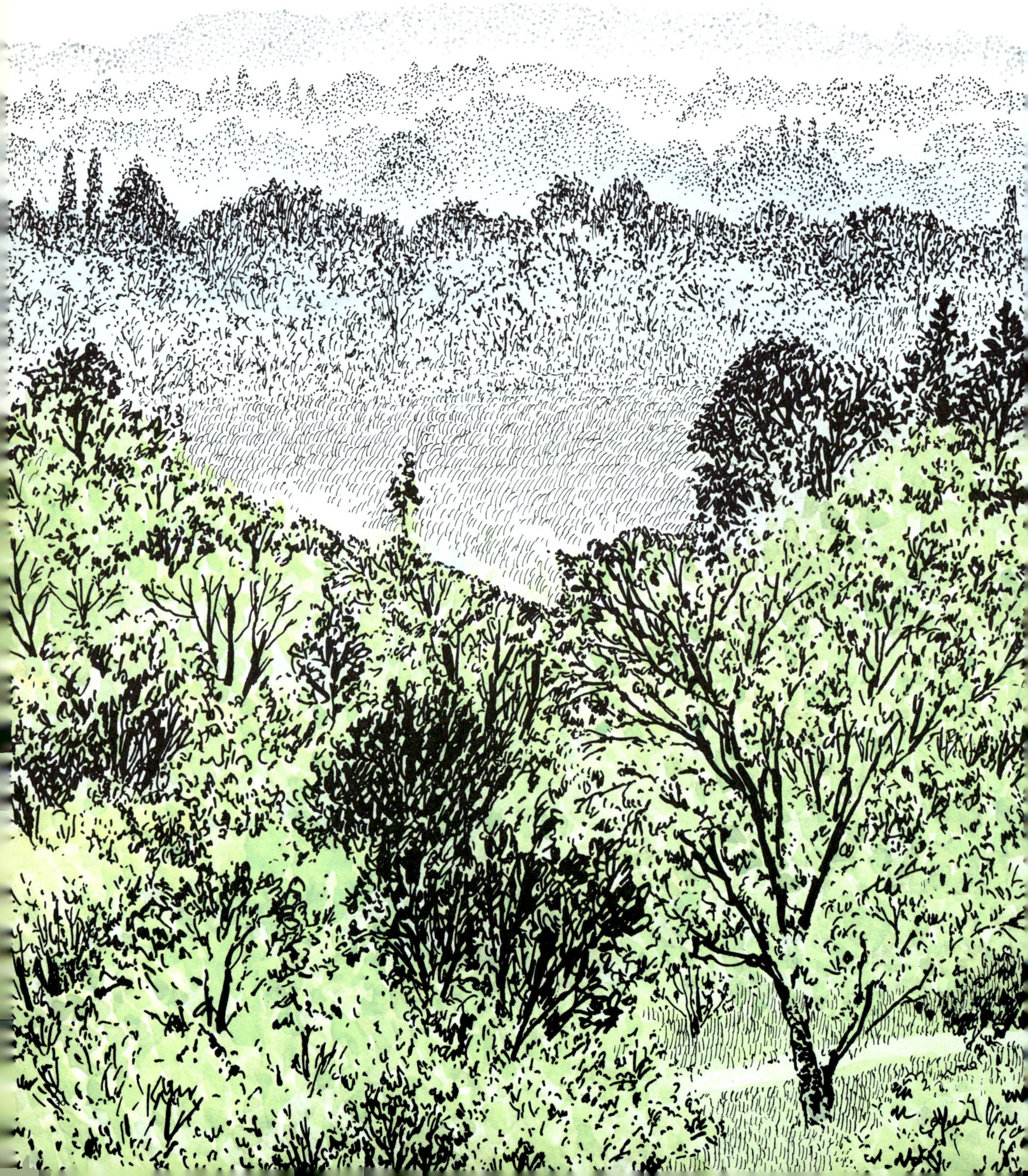

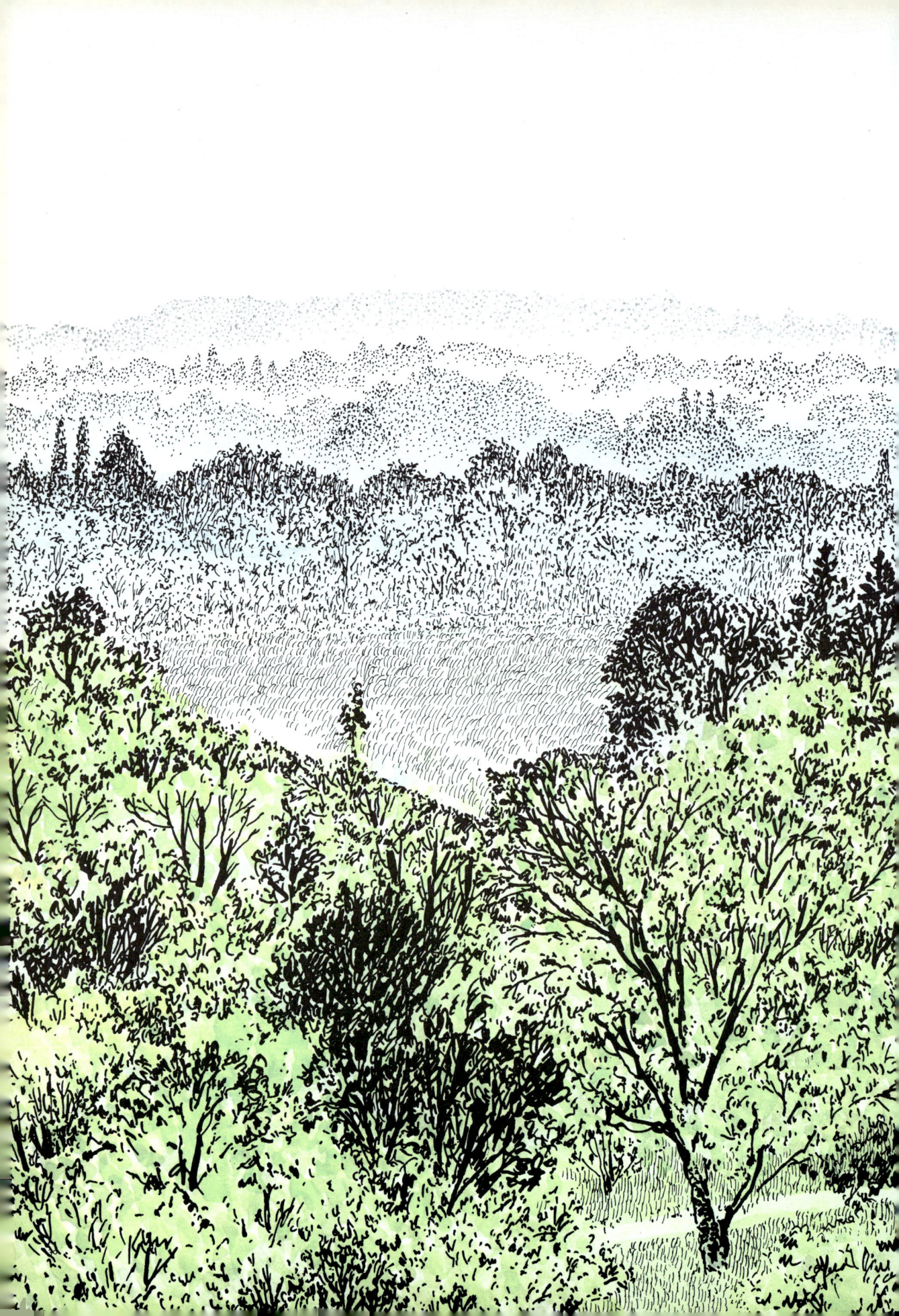

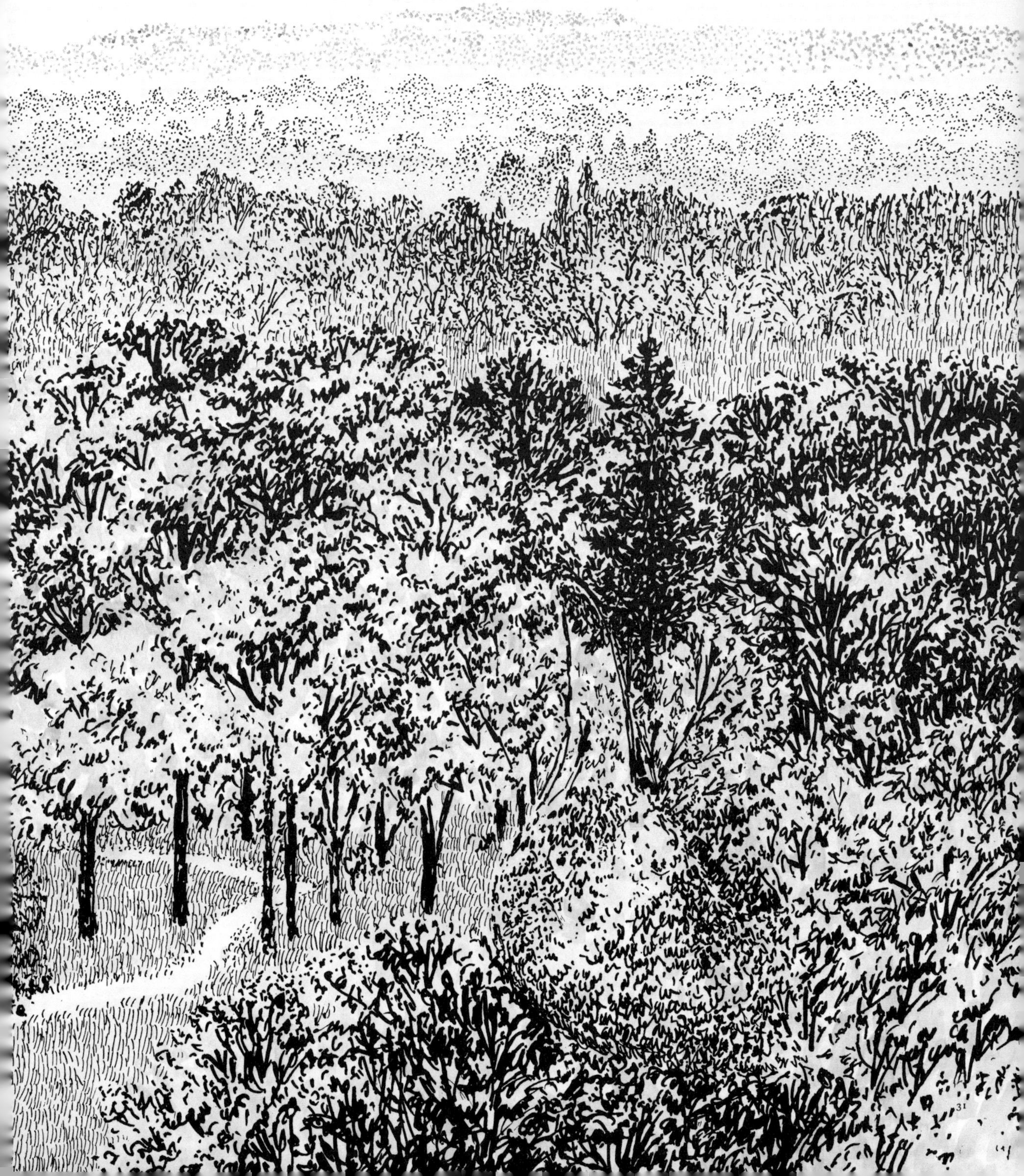

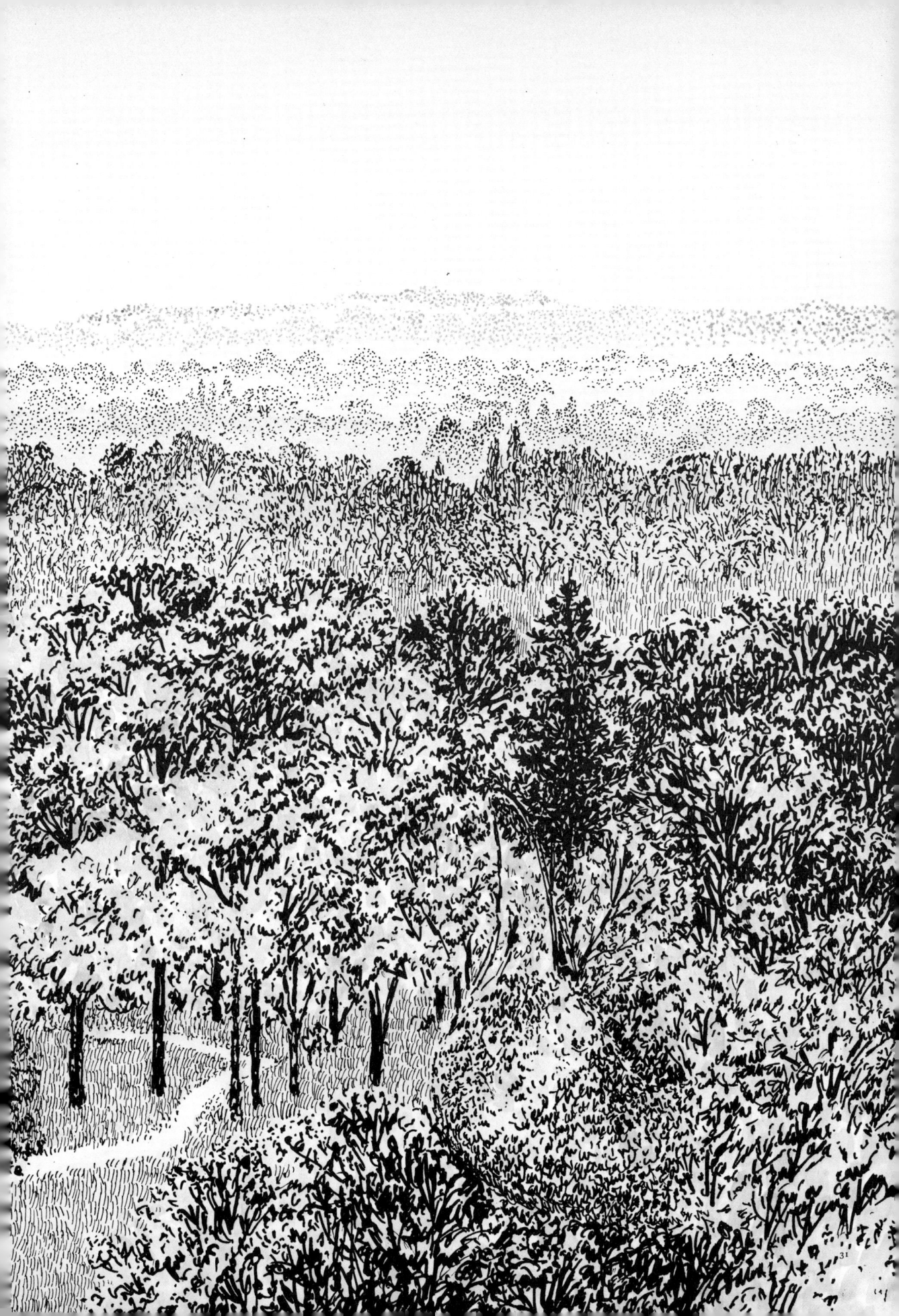

There are many animals and birds hidden in every page of *Anno's Animals*. Here are some clues to help you find some of them but you will be able to identify many more for yourself. Here and there you may even discover that there are people hiding, too . . .

Cover: rabbit, turtle.

pp 2–3: crowned crane, rhinoceros, lynx, squirrel.

4–5: elephant, camel, pig, rabbit, ant-eater, baboon, wild boar.

6–7: owl, crane, seal, goat, kid, parrot.

8–9: cockatoo, reindeer, moose, monkey, dog, egret, stork.

10–11: tiger, bat, goose, goat, cow, rat.

12–13: reindeer, godwit, bison, wild boar, toucan, goose.

14–15: dove, ostrich, mandarin duck, penguin, crow, cat.

16–17: dog, donkey, frog, hippopotamus, rooster, owl, squirrel, leopard.

18–19: horse, wolf, two bears, lion, fish.

20–21: panda, snail, lion, giraffe, cat, raccoon, mole, porcupine, zebra, flamingo, koala, dog, buffalo, skunk.

22–23: cheetah, gorilla, rhinoceros, deer.

24–25: stork, bear, pelican, giraffe, fox, llama.

26–27: chimpanzee, raccoon, lizard, reindeer, rabbit, kangaroo.

28–29: jackal, hornbill, scorpion, peregrine falcon, jaguar, armadillo, two ants.

30–31: duck.